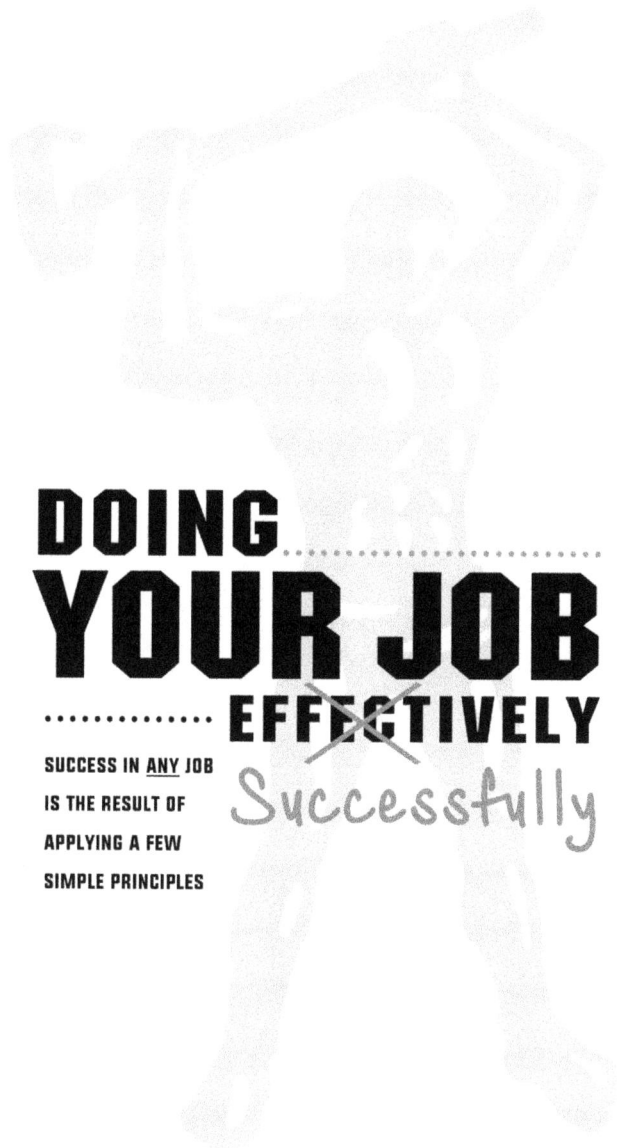

DOING YOUR JOB

~~EFFECTIVELY~~ Successfully

SUCCESS IN <u>ANY</u> JOB IS THE RESULT OF APPLYING A FEW SIMPLE PRINCIPLES

TAB EDWARDS

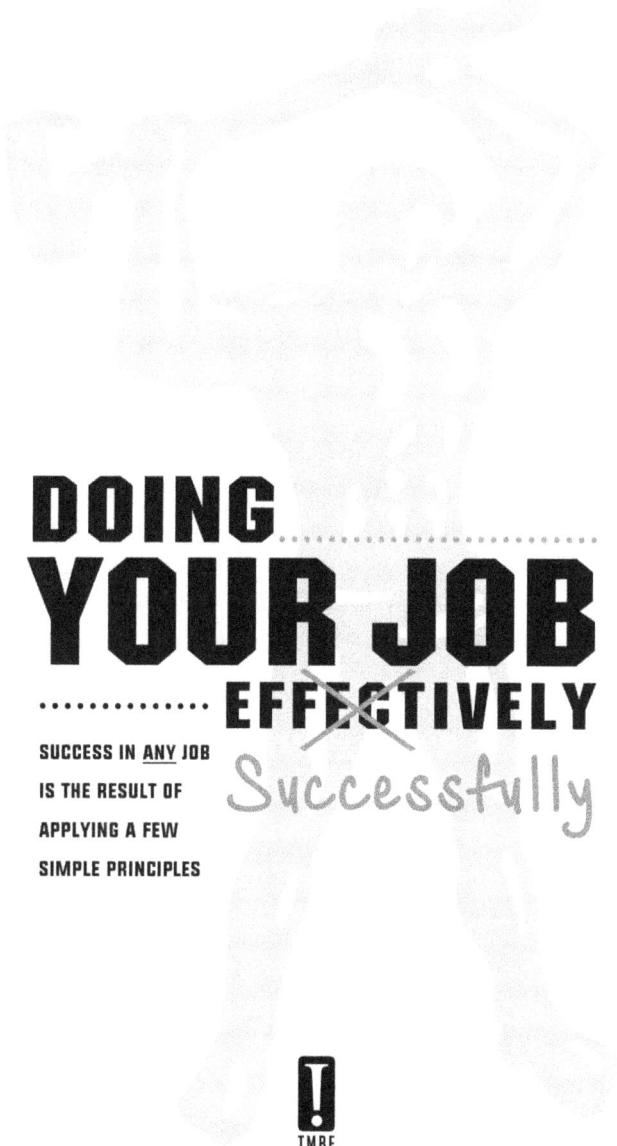

DOING YOUR JOB

EFFECTIVELY ~~EFFECTIVELY~~ *Successfully*

**SUCCESS IN <u>ANY</u> JOB
IS THE RESULT OF
APPLYING A FEW
SIMPLE PRINCIPLES**

!

TMBE

TMBE**MEDIA**, PHILADELPHIA, PENNSYLVANIA 19129

TMBE / *Media*

ISBN 978-0-9909866-7-6

This publication is designed to provide authoritative information in regards to the subject matter covered. It is sold with the understanding that the publisher is not engaged in rendering legal, accounting, or other professional services. If legal advice or other expert assistance is required, the services of a competent professional person should be sought.

—From a declaration of principles jointly adopted by a committee of the American Bar Association and a committee of publishers.

Tab Edwards books are available at special quantity discounts to use as premiums and promotions, or for use in corporate training programs. For more information, please visit the website www.TabEdwards.com.

Designed by Water Creative
Philadelphia, PA.

1   3   5   7   9   10   8   6   4   2

TTX

CONTENTS

C

CONCLUSION
[221]

You are accountable for your own job success

A

ABOUT THE AUTHOR
[229]

Tab Edwards: consultant, best-selling author, speaker, educator

E

ENGAGEMENT
[231]

Helping organizations, teams, and individuals improve performance and achieve success

A

APPENDIX
[237]

The Job-Success Plan Workbook and the Job-Success Plan Checklist

INTRODUCTION

In the summer of 2016, a Philadelphia-based hospital invited me to deliver a seminar on the topic of Human Capital Strategy and Employee Engagement to a gathering of hospital administrators, nursing staff, managers, and other hospital associates who held various positions within the hospital.

While speaking on the topic of employee engagement (the extent to which employees commit to something or someone in their organization, how hard they work, how well they perform, and how long they may stay as a result of that commitment), I began to discuss how everyone in an organization holds a specific job that was created for the purpose of helping the organization succeed. I shared that every job within an organization has been created to contribute something that the organization has determined is necessary for that organization to thrive; every job is valuable.

Excluding cases of nepotism or cronyism (creating unnecessary jobs or giving jobs to friends and family members without taking into consideration their qualifications), each job within an organization should be created to perform activities, such that, by successfully doing so, the holder of that job will contribute his or her share toward helping the organization accomplish its goals and deliver on its mission. And when the job-holder can see the relationship between the activities s/he performs in the course of doing his or her job and the contribution and impact those actions have on an organization's prosperity, the job-holder becomes more engaged and feels valued and overall better (and prouder) about the job s/he does.

This specific topic of the seminar generated lots of interesting discussion, most focused around how the nursing staff in attendance felt undervalued and how the things that I shared with the audience relating to "feeling valued" resonated with them. In the midst of the open discussion, I noticed that one person was sitting quietly in the rear of the room with a demeanor that suggested she felt that she either didn't belong in this session or that she couldn't relate to the things that I was sharing or the things that were being discussed by audience members.

When the ad-hoc conversations slowed, I asked the woman about her thoughts on the things that were being discussed. She said, "Um. I don't know. I just feel like these things don't apply to me," to which I replied, "Why do you feel that way?" She said that she felt that way because she was "only a Medical Front Desk Receptionist" and that her job was not as "important" as everyone else's in the room.

I remember thinking how unfortunate it was that the woman felt as though her job as a Medical Receptionist was somehow insignificant. I also remember thinking how difficult it must be to get up every morning to arrive to work at 7:00AM and, once you get there, to feel as though you – as an extension of your job – are somehow unimportant when compared to, say, an RN Unit Manager.

After the woman openly shared her personal feelings on the matter, I asked her a follow up question. I asked: "What is your job?" The woman replied, "As I just said, I am a Medical Front Desk Receptionist," to which I replied, "No, I mean, what is your *job*?" And she replied, "I just told you, I am a *Medical Front Desk Receptionist.*" I said, "Yes, I understand. Your position and job title is that of Medical Front Desk Receptionist, but what do you actually *do*?"

The woman sheepishly described her job responsibilities: "I only answer the phones. I sign people in and out, and I accept deliveries. See, like I said, my job is not that important."

I then asked the woman a very simple question designed to enable her to begin to appreciate the value of the work that she does. I asked, "Ok. So what would happen if you got stuck in traffic on a very snowy day and arrived at work 2 hours late?" After a pause, the woman described the consequences of her arriving late to work: "Well, [sigh], important packages and deliveries may not get signed for, visitors and patients would get angry about having to wait in the lobby. They'd file complaints, and everyone would be upset ..."

I then asked an additional series of almost diagnostic questions, including: "And what would be the impact of important packages and deliveries not getting to their destinations within the hospital?" To this question, many people in attendance chimed in with answers of their own, ranging from, "If they are things needed for the physicians to provide care, then it could negatively impact the patient. It could also adversely affect the hospital's quality of care ratings." Another participant added, "If a sick patient needs to see a health care practitioner and is left waiting in the lobby for 2 hours, then there could be life-threatening consequences." Someone else chimed in, "Oh my God! I couldn't imagine what chaos that would cause in the lobby!"

At that point, it was becoming obvious that the woman was starting to feel more confident that her job – and by extension, she – was valuable to the hospital in ways that she hadn't ever considered.

To reinforce the woman's visible growth in confidence, I shared the results of a study that had been published a few months earlier in an April 2016 issue of the *Journal of Medical Practice Management*. The study of nearly 35,000 healthcare practices found that the front-desk staff and the level of customer service they provided was the #1 patient complaint. These complaints can spread virally and negatively impact a healthcare provider's reputation and even its business; everyone in attendance nodded their heads in knowing confirmation.

I then went to the whiteboard and drew a flow diagram that illustrated the domino-effect of life at the hospital if the woman was away from her job for a couple of hours: Important packages would potentially not be signed for; physicians would not be able to deliver the highest quality of care; the hospital's Hospital Compare overall rating (the comprehensive rating of how well each hospital performs, on average, compared with other U.S. hospitals) would be negatively impacted; patients with a choice of providers may use a different hospital; fewer hospital beds would be filled; there would be lower reimbursements; the hospital would have a reduced ability to accomplish its goals; and finally, there would be the potential that the hospital would have an unsuccessful year.

Sure, some of the links in the aforementioned chain of events stretch things a bit. However, I wanted to make the point that *everyone's* job in an organization has value, and it is up to the organization's leadership to ensure that every associate from the mail room to the C-suite understands the value that their job contributes to the organization's success. More importantly, at least as it relates to employee engagement, every worker should be able to see exactly how the things they do translate into organizational performance.

As the discussion wound down, the Medical Front Desk Receptionist ended by saying, "I want to say 'Thank you all' for helping me realize that I'm not *just* a Front Desk Receptionist. I not only see how important my job is, but I also have a better understanding of how important it is for me to do *my* part, no matter how small I think it might be in the grand scheme of things, to help the hospital run efficiently and be the best that it can be." Applause erupted throughout the room!

Of everything that was discussed related to the woman's job and its significance to the hospital, the one thing that stuck with me was the last thing she said, "…I also have a better understanding of how important it is for me to do *my* part …"

I wondered: Why did it take ME to demonstrate and explain the relationship between the woman's job and the hospital's success? Shouldn't everyone have a clear understanding of (1) their job responsibilities; (2) how these responsibilities are (should be) designed such that, if they are completed, the worker would achieve measurable objectives defined for them during the course of the year; (3) how, as the worker achieves his or her job-related work objectives, they contribute to their department's and, ultimately, the organization's success; and (4) how valuable they are to the organization?

Prior to that seminar, the Medical Front Desk Receptionist – by all indications – simply went about her day performing a series of tasks without appreciating their value or even understanding which of the performed tasks were more important than others. By the end of the seminar, however, the woman had established a commitment to do her job better "… to help the hospital run efficiently and be the best that it could be."

The woman committed to do her job better than she had been doing it prior to the seminar, because she now appreciated how important it was to not simply perform her defined job duties, but to perform them with the highest quality. She no longer wanted to simply *do her job*. She now wanted to perform her job to the best degree possible. By doing so, she believed that she would be doing her part to help the hospital succeed.

She realized that her job was more than simply answering phones, accepting packages, signing people in and out, and carrying out other administrative activities; her job, she now believes, is to help the hospital succeed. She realized that to perform her job to the degree necessary to support the hospital's success, it would require her to perform more and different activities than those defined in her job description. By doing that, she surmised, she would not only help the hospital better succeed, but she would also develop new skills, making her a better employee and professional. Now, she acknowledged, she knows exactly what her job *really* is.

The journey and awakening of the Medical Front Desk Receptionist made me wonder how many people actually *know* what their job is ...

START >>

1

CHAPTER**ONE**

WHAT, EXACTLY, *IS* YOUR JOB, ANYWAY?

Why were you hired by your organization?

It all started when your organization identified a specific job-need that required filling. The exact need which prompted the organization to search for a candidate for the job will be discussed a bit later. However, for now, let's just assume that there is a legitimate need within the organization; a need that can be satisfied by hiring a good candidate with the requisite skills to perform the job requirements.

To find the right candidate for the job, your organization entered the recruiting phase of the hiring process, reaching out to a pool of candidates with the skills and experience necessary to successfully perform the job. They entered the tedious recruitment process of posting the job on the organization's and external websites, soliciting referrals, placing help wanted advertisements, participating in college campus recruitment, scouring social media sites, and carrying out other recruiting outreach efforts.

Eventually, after months of sifting through resumes and job applications, becoming numb from asking those same ol' lame interview questions from the 1950s, such as, "Where do you see yourself five years from now?" (to which the interviewee is undoubtedly thinking to him or herself "at my *next* job after this one"), and debating with your fellow Talent Recruitment colleagues, they believe they have found their candidate. You!

The organization's representatives call to inform you of the good news: They want to offer you the job! After verbally accepting the offer, you jump for joy and let out a big "YEAH!" which prompts those seated near you to ask, "Hey, why all the excitement?" You answer, "I just got offered a great new job!" After a few minutes of "Congratulations!" and joyous celebration, someone in the room asks the $64 dollar question: "What, exactly, *is* your new job anyway?"

Have you ever been asked this question or really thought about it? If not, you might find that properly answering it is more difficult than you could have imagined. Give it a try:

In the box below, write down your answer to the question "What *is* your job?"

If you are like most people in the workforce, your answer to the question, "What is your job?" might be something like "I am an analyst," or "my job is to educate kids," or "my job is to fix the fleet of company cars when they break." Or your response might be "my job is to sell my company's goods and services," or even "my job is to score points, touchdowns." And if, for instance, you reply that "I am an attorney," a logical follow-up question would be, "And what exactly do you *do* as an attorney?"

Questions such as "What is your job?" are so ambiguous that most people, I suspect, would respond with an answer that is likewise both general and ambiguous, such as "I am an attorney." Why? It could be that the person thinks that the questioner is only asking to make polite conversation and is not *really* interested in the person's work. So the person responds with an equally-general-yet-polite answer: I am an attorney.

You might find that some percentage of the respondents – who are really into their jobs and take pride in the actual work they do – might go a step further and add some context, such as, "I am a mechanic, and my job is to fix the fleet of company cars when they break. By fixing the cars, I help the sales representatives get to and from their client appointments without hassle."

Based on 30 years of experience working with organizations and their employees to help them become more effective at accomplishing goals and achieving objectives, I have found that, when asked about their job, virtually no worker provides an answer that really gets at the heart of the job they have been hired to do: help their organization *succeed* (however "success" is defined); I know this because I always ask the question.

POSITION VS. JOB

At times, when working with an organization's workers, I truly wonder whether or not the workers truly *know* why they were hired and, therefore, what their jobs *really* are. Most workers meld the *position* they were hired into with the *job* they were hired to do, and erroneously think they are one and the same.

A worker's *position* is simply a description of where that person fits within the organization's structure, and each position is given a name or title to help others identify exactly where that person fits within the organization's framework. For example, the position of the person who sits at the head of the organization is commonly assigned the title of "Chief," meaning leader or ruler, as in *Chief Executive Officer* (CEO). When someone describes herself as the CEO, everyone knows the position that the person holds within their organization: she sits at the top. And, if someone holds the position of "Receptionist," then the expectation (based solely on the worker's assigned position) is that the person can be found sitting at the entrance to an office space; he is the first person who greets you when you walk through the entrance.

For those who are not familiar with organizational or company dynamics, the distinction between *position* and *job* can more easily be understood by using sports – in this case, American football – as an example.

Each football team has eleven of its players on the field at the same time; one team plays offense (trying to score points), whereas the other team plays defense (trying to stop the other team's offense from scoring). Each team's players line up on either side of where the play will start; this starting line is called the *line of scrimmage*.

Each player is assigned to a certain *position* on the field. The position primarily designates where that player lines up on the field and indicates his responsibilities. The "center," for example, lines up in the *center* of his team's formation, with players flanked to his right and left. Another player is called the "quarterback." The quarterback is the player who sets up directly behind the center, a *quarter* of the way *back* (or, a "quarter-back") between the line of scrimmage and the player on his team that is furthest from the line of scrimmage who is called the "full-back." The quarterback is the player who puts his hands between the legs of the center, receives the football, and sets the play in motion.

So, when someone watches a football game, that person will know exactly where the quarterback and the center are positioned, and they will also have an idea about the activities that each player is responsible for based solely on the name of the position to which the player has been assigned.

As the above-provided example illustrates, gaining an understanding of a worker's *position* within an organization is not very difficult; a worker's or a football player's *position* is simply a descriptor of where that person fits within the organization's or team's structure, and the general activities they are responsible for carrying out on a daily basis. However, understanding someone's *job*, well, that's a bit more complex, and requires more investigation.

WHY YOU WERE HIRED

Simply put: you were hired to do a *job*. But, what does that actually *mean*?

To help you fully appreciate why organizations hire workers and what the workers are actually hired to do, I will start by asking three seemingly-basic questions:

1. What should workers in an organization *do*?
2. Why should the workers do what you suggested in your answer to question #1?
3. How will the workers know *what* to do to satisfy your answer to question #1?

An organization's leader who cannot properly answer these three basic questions is likely managing by the seat of his or her pants. And a leader who *can* answer these questions will most certainly answer question #3 with, "The workers' activities will be directed at realizing initiatives aimed at accomplishing strategy goals." I will examine these questions in greater detail to shed light on the importance of workers' efforts being focused on achieving objectives and accomplishing goals.

Question #1: What should workers in an organization do?

In short, workers should perform *productive activities.* Productive activities are those which make things, bring things into existence, accomplish something particular, or *cause something to happen.*

In a capitalistic economic system – an economic system in which the means of production and capital goods are owned and sold by private individuals or businesses for profit – the basic *labor-to-wealth model* described below is common within a capitalistic *enterprise*:

1. The enterprise owner seeks capital wealth;

2. The owner identifies goods with "use-value" and "exchange-value;"

3. The owner defines processes to create and sell goods;

4. The owner hires workers to perform a task (labor) necessary to create and sell the goods, ultimately delivering wealth;

5. Labor is divided by skill, and workers follow defined processes to produce and sell the goods. The *division of labor* is a specific mode of cooperation wherein different tasks are assigned to different people based on the tasks needed to produce a specific good;

6. Goods, which have "use-value," are sold to buyers. "Use-value" means that a good must have properties that allow it to satisfy some human need or want;

7. Buyers pay the owner for the goods which have an "exchange-value" (worth exchanging for something of equal value, e.g. money); and

8. The owner of the enterprise acquires capital wealth.

Workers in this capitalistic model are hired to perform *productive work*: work that produces goods with use- and exchange-value. In *Capital: A Critique of Political Economy*, German philosopher Karl Marx wrote that productive activity (which he called "the useful character of the labor") is simply the expenditure of human labor power performing qualitatively different productive activities.

"Productive activity" begets productivity. The application of labor brings about some desired outcome (goal). Productive activity is activity (a worker's labor) that contributes to the achievement of business objectives and goals. In a capitalistic system, that goal is most often what Marx calls "capitalist wealth." He wrote:

> The utility of a thing makes it a use-value. The use-values, coat, linen, etc., *i.e.*, the bodies of commodities, are combinations of two elements – matter and labor. In the use-value of each commodity there is contained useful labor, *i.e.*, productive activity of a definite kind and **exercised with a definite aim**.

The coat, in the example below, is a use-value item that satisfies a particular consumer want. Its existence is the result of a worker's productive activity, the nature of which is determined by its aim. Put differently, **workers' activities are determined by specific goals**.

YOUR JOB: CONTRIBUTE TO THE OWNER'S GOALS

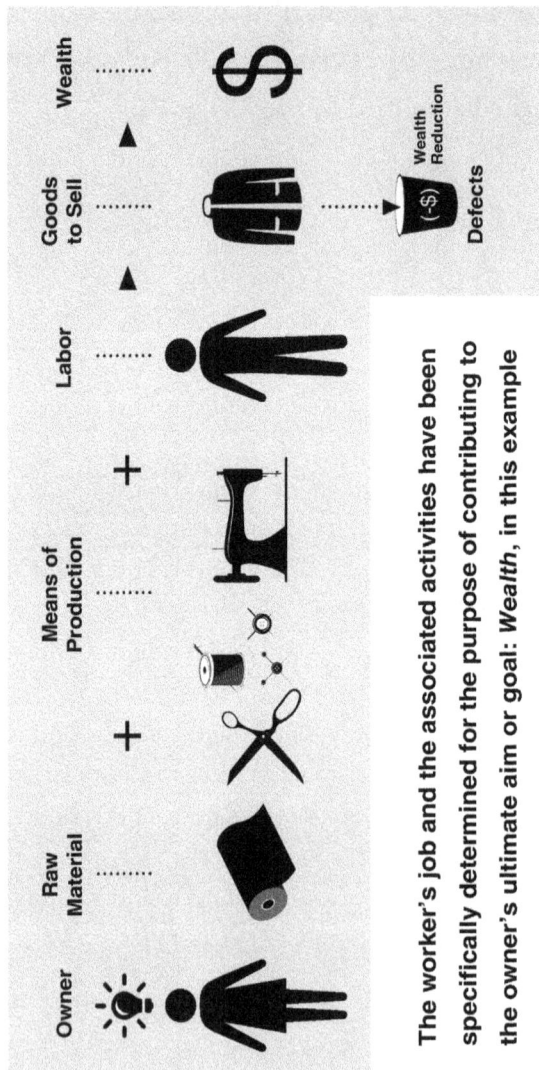

| Owner | Raw Material | + | Means of Production | + | Labor | ▲ | Goods to Sell | ▲ | Wealth |

Wealth Reduction

Defects

(-$)

The worker's job and the associated activities have been specifically determined for the purpose of contributing to the owner's ultimate aim or goal: *Wealth*, in this example

Question #2: Why should the workers do what you suggest in your answer to question #1?

The simple answer is because they are *paid* for their productive activity or labor.

Payment – if the wage is fair – is an equitable exchange for their labor. Another reason, although slightly less compelling, is because work provides them with a sense of accomplishment. This is important to the human psyche.

Americans who are not in the workforce are the most likely group to be depressed. While it is fair to question whether the lack of work leads to depression or whether being depressed contributes to the lack of work, the point remains: when people are involuntarily unemployed, they have a tendency to be more depressed than those who are gainfully employed. This is the conclusion of a 2013 survey conducted by the *Gallup-Healthways Well-Being Index*. It found that 16.6% of unemployed Americans are depressed compared with 5.6% of those who work full time. Gallup controlled for 12 variables: age, gender, income, education, race and ethnicity, marital status, having children, region, employment status, obesity, having health insurance, and being a caregiver, so that they could examine each factor independently to find out which is most strongly linked to depression.

"Self-esteem and self-worth are closely aligned with working," says psychotherapist Charles Allen, author of

Why Good People Make Bad Choices. When you have a job, you are a contributing member of society, which gives you a sense of value and self-worth. This is consistent with psychologist Abraham Maslow's hierarchy of needs. He argues that people will be unfulfilled until they have first satisfied basic physiological needs, such as hunger, and important needs, such as safety and security (including work), and "esteem needs," which can come from achievement and the respect of others. To remain gainfully-employed and to continue receiving the fulfilling benefits that employment can help bring, it is requisite that the worker performs the tasks, activities, and functions that s/he has been hired to perform, and to perform them to an excellent level.

Question #3: How will the workers know **what** to do to satisfy your answer to question #1?

Workers are hired to perform specific tasks, activities, and functions related to what the employer is trying to accomplish. In this case, if the employer is ultimately trying to increase her wealth, and the means of wealth creation for this employer are the production and sale of goods, then the worker will be hired to perform specific tasks, activities, and functions related to the production or sale of goods. In the most astute organizations, these specific tasks, activities, functions, and expected results are documented in workers' job descriptions and performance plans. These then serve as a guide for the workers to ensure that they perform productive work. This will be discussed in greater detail in *Chapter 4: The Anatomy of Job Success*.

What the worker must *specifically* do is determined by the processes that were set up to produce and sell the goods which are necessary for the capitalist to accomplish his or her goal of accumulating wealth. In the simplistic labor-to-wealth model previously introduced, stage #5 is the stage at which workers learn exactly what they must do. In other words, *workers follow the defined processes to produce and sell goods.*

A "job," therefore, is a set of related tasks, responsibilities, and actions to be undertaken to produce or realize some desired end (e.g. achieving individual goals and objectives that contribute to organizational success). Ultimately, and in the strictest sense, **workers' activities (their *jobs*) have been specifically determined to contribute to the owner's ultimate aim or goal, and for nothing else.**

After having read the contents of this chapter, *now* use the box below to write down what your job is.

If your description contains content related to *helping your organization achieve its objectives, accomplish its goals,* or simply *to be successful,* then congratulations! You have taken the first step toward performing your job – whatever it is – successfully.

I want to acknowledge that not all jobs and positions that workers hold within organizations are directed toward building an owner's capital wealth. Many organizations, such as state, local, and government agencies, non-profit and not-for-profit organizations, and other such entities have altruistic and/or other non-capital-wealth-related missions. The value they deliver is almost always different than that of for-profit organizations.

Hospitals, for example, may have a mission to improve the health of the communities they support. Schools might have an aim to provide quality experiences that foster a child's well-being. And religious institutions might have a goal to alleviate human suffering and satisfy human needs. That said, whatever an organization's ultimate aim, the job of the hired workers will be to contribute to the mission, goals, and/or success of that organization, however the organization defines success.

2

CHAPTER**TWO**

WHAT IS "SUCCESS"?
SPECIFICALLY, WHAT IS "JOB-SUCCESS"?

This was the setting for what turned into a discussion of expectations and the possible consequences of not meeting those expectations. It began with [National Football League head coach Mike] Tomlin being asked, "When you don't reach your goal of getting to the postseason ..." only to have Tomlin interrupt with, "Getting to the postseason is not my goal. My goal is to win the World Championship."

– An excerpt from
"Steelers Nation is the Ultimate Motivator,"
at Steelers.com

Recently, I worked with a $135 billion U.S.-based corporation on developing and implementing an employee "effectiveness" program as part of their human capital strategy. Specifically, the initiative was based on a planned human capital investment designed to improve employee effectiveness in generating revenue, attracting and retaining clients, and improving overall performance – the organization's *goals.*

At the initial planning meeting which was attended by the company's President and other senior executives, the assembled masses began to rattle off a list of investments that might be made in upgrading employee effectiveness and, ultimately, job performance. After about 90 minutes of discussion, I asked a fundamental (and, surprisingly) conversation-stopping question: "What do we consider to be an 'effective' employee in each of the positions in question?"

Silence.

It seemed that everyone had a definitive opinion of the types of investments that could be made in upgrading employee effectiveness – MBA degrees for executives, HiPos, and Key Talent; Challenger training for sales reps; coaching tools for managers; technology upgrades; organization redesign; and the list went on – but no one bothered to define what an effective employee looked like or to validate whether any of the proposed investments would yield the intended results of improving an associate's job effectiveness. We were putting our shoes on before the socks: How could we know which investments to make without knowing what investments were needed?

I offered that until we defined what we wanted to achieve via the work of associates (organizational goals or desired outcomes) and took an honest inventory of talent we currently had and their current measure of effectiveness at achieving their individual goals and objectives, we could not know what effectiveness-improvement-measures were needed. The fundamental starting point was to specifically define what we considered an *effective* employee to be and the associated attributes of effectiveness.

EFFECTIVENESS

The word *effective* functions as an adjective; it hinges on whether or not an intended function is performed. It does not necessarily focus on *how* something is done, but rather, if it is done at all. For example, if I hired a high school student to paint my shed, and the student painted it on-time and on-budget – albeit sloppily and not as I desired – that student would be considered to have effectively painted my shed. Effective, in this example, is simply the student's ability to complete the task assigned to him or her. The fact that the student completed the job on-time and on-budget simply means that he did his job effectively and efficiently (on-time and on-budget), not necessarily acceptably.

Suppose you wanted to lose weight – 20 pounds, to be exact – and you saw a television commercial advertising a fat-burning pill, "Super Pounds Off." The commercial (as they all do) made the benefits of the Super Pounds Off pills sound wonderful, so you ordered a 30-day supply. The commercial gave the impression that if you simply took the pills for 30 days, you would lose ridiculous amounts of weight, while maintaining your current eating habits … no less!

Your Super Pounds Off pills arrive and you begin the regimen as prescribed on the label. At the end of the 30-day period, you weigh yourself on the scale and found that by taking the fat-burning pills as instructed, you lost ½ pound. Would you consider the pills to have been *effective*? The answer could be "yes" or "no," depending on how you define "effective." If by "effective" you mean that the pills performed their intended function of helping you lose weight, then one could make the argument that the pills were in fact effective. If, however, your weight-loss goal was to lose 20 pounds by taking the Super Pounds Off pills, then the pills would be considered to have been ineffective because they did not help you to accomplish the goal for which you purchased and used them.

This raises the issue of *the determinants* of effectiveness. On the surface, when we hear that someone has completed a task effectively, we automatically assume that the person has done a good job completing the task; in actuality, that is not always the case. When I hired the student to paint my shed, did I have certain expectations about the quality I expected from the paint job? Did I clearly define those quality expectations with the student, including the criteria I would use to gauge job quality and, therefore, the student's job effectiveness?

One's job effectiveness (how well they performed in completing the assigned job) may be impacted by several things, many of which are outside the worker's control. These factors may include the organization's strategy and whether or not the relevant elements of the strategy have been cascaded down to the associate and included in the associate's performance plan; the worker's job workflow process and the (in)efficiencies contained therein; and the technology and systems used by the worker in performing his or her job, to name just a few.

This begs the question: how do you know that a person has *effectively* completed a task or performed a job? As you begin to consider the parameters, criteria, and metrics that will be used to determine one's job effectiveness, you start to move away from discussing job effectiveness per-se (i.e. whether or not the worker simply completed the defined task), and move into considering job *execution*.

The most important aspect of a strategic plan or strategy is *execution*

"Execution" relates to the *successful* performance of necessary activities to deliver the desired outcome(s) of an engagement, project, a plan, or a strategy, whereas *success* is determined by the accomplishment of goals and the achievement of objectives defined for the engagement, the project, the plan, or the strategy.

Success is the desired, and even necessary, end-state. It signifies the achievement of what an organization has defined as being necessary to fulfill its mission, deliver value to its stakeholders, to prosper, to thrive, to survive, or heck, even to just keep the lights on!

Organizational performance is effectively executing the strategic plan (i.e. strategy) defined by the organization for the purpose of, among other things, improving performance, delivering value, and creating a sustainable competitive advantage. Put differently, a worker's job performance is determined by the worker's effectiveness at accomplishing the tasks and initiatives related to and required to successfully achieve the individual's work objectives and to accomplish his or her goals.

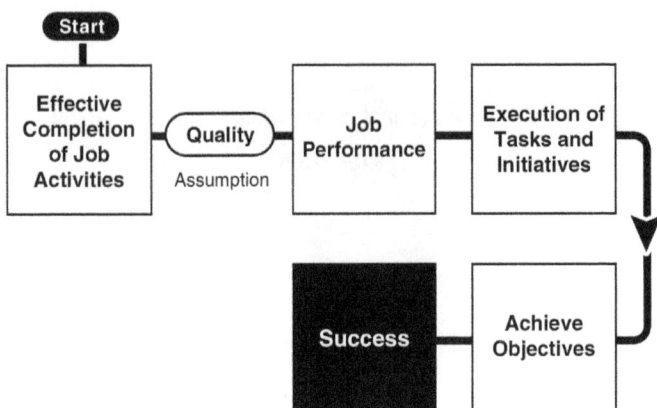

WHAT IS "SUCCESS?"
WHAT DOES IT MEAN TO BE *SUCCESSFUL*?

By its most basic definition, to *succeed* is to attain some desired object or pre-defined end. By this definition, "success" could be defined as one's ability to accomplish a defined goal or achieve a specific objective. Put differently, success is the ability to have attained or achieved some defined outcome or end. Success, therefore, is the act of having attained some desired end or achieved some desired outcome.

All professional sports teams and athletes competing in individual events want to accomplish their #1 goal of winning their sport's championship. If American gymnast Simone Biles, the 2016 Olympic gold medalist in three events (the individual all-around, vault, and floor exercise) had set a goal to win the Olympic gold medal in the balance beam event (an event in which she ultimately won the bronze medal), her performance in that event could be seen by her as unsuccessful. Were it not for a slip on the balance beam, she might have actually won the gold medal, which suggests that her performance in the event was still pretty good.

So while Biles did not win the gold medal, she felt that she performed well enough to feel good about the performance. "The rest of the routine was still pretty good, so I can't be too disappointed in myself," Biles said after the Olympic women's balance beam final. And when you consider that there are 5.4 million people who participate in gymnastics in the U.S., (according to Statista) to finish third means that Biles was still better than at least 99.9999% of everyone else, not just in the U.S., but in the world. Within this context, anyone would consider winning a bronze medal at the Olympics to be a rare achievement and an unqualified success. If Biles measured her success in the balance beam event based on the definition of success offered by John Wooden, the legendary UCLA basketball coach who was known for winning a remarkable ten NCAA championships in twelve years, then an argument could be made that she was, indeed, successful. Wooden said that success is "peace of mind attained only through self-satisfaction in knowing you made the effort to do the best of which you're capable." Given Biles' post-event comments that "The rest of the routine was still pretty good, so I can't be too disappointed in myself," then, from that perspective (shared with Wooden), maybe she did succeed.

That said, *by strict definition*, however, if Biles had established the goal of winning the gold medal in the balance beam event, she would have been unsuccessful, having fallen short of accomplishing her pre-defined goal.

PERSONAL GOALS AND PROFESSIONAL (JOB-RELATED) GOALS

John Wooden's definition of success raises an interesting point to consider: personal goals vs. job-related work goals.

Personally-defined goals, such as. "My name is Bob, and I want to get a 'B' grade on my next science test," or "I want to find happiness in a relationship" are specific to the person defining the goals and may not be suitable for anyone else. If, for example, Bob's classmate, Susan, takes the same test as Bob and scores a "B" on the test, she might be disappointed that she did not perform better. For Bob, getting a "B" on the test means he can run home and celebrate the good news with his family. Susan, on the other hand, will run straight to the library to study harder for the next science test.

The highest typing speed ever recorded was 216 words per minute, a record documented in 1946. More recently, the fastest recorded typing speed of 212 words per minute was achieved by Barbara Blackburn during a test in 2005 – using a typewriter!

Suppose that Mike, whose current typing speed is 190 words per minute, established a goal "to achieve a typing speed of 213 words per minute." After taking the typing test, he achieved a speed of 208 words per minute, Mike would feel great. Even though he fell short (i.e. was unsuccessful) at achieving his pre-defined goal of 213 words per minute, he was thoroughly pleased that his speed had improved 18 words per minute, meaning that he had become a much better typist. It would appear that Mike subscribes to the idea that "success" is more about the journey than the end result.

These examples illustrate the difference between personal goals and job-related work goals. Personal goals are often fluid, and, depending on the satisfaction the goal-setter receives from the results of his or her efforts at pursuing the defined goal, the goal-setter could be perfectly satisfied, even though, strictly speaking, he or she was unsuccessful at accomplishing the defined goal.

Job-related work goals are more constant than personally-defined goals.

Consider the following example. You work for a tree removal company that recently won a contract to clear 100 trees from a section of forest that is being developed as a paved throughway for automobile travel. One contract condition is that all 100 trees must be removed by next Friday for your company to receive the full contract amount of $100,000. If the company cannot remove all 100 trees as contracted, then the company will only be paid $75,000.

Suppose, for example, your boss defined a work objective for you to chop down ten trees by next Friday. If you are successful at your job and are able to cut down the ten trees, then it would result in the company receiving its $100,000 payment. Because of your success, you would receive a $2,000 bonus. If, however, by the end of the Friday contract period, you were only able to chop down seven trees, your company would fall short of its goal of removing 100 trees and would not earn the full $100,000 payment. As a result, the company loses $25,000, you miss out on a $2,000 bonus, and your boss rates your job performance as "Not meeting expectations" and "Needs Improvement."

You were hired to do a specific job with clearly-defined responsibilities: chop down ten trees within a given, realistic timeframe. If you were successful in performing your job, then your success would have contributed to your company's success, and both you and the company would have reaped the rewards of that success. However, because you did not perform your job successfully, neither you nor your company accomplished your respective goals and the company's wealth was diminished.

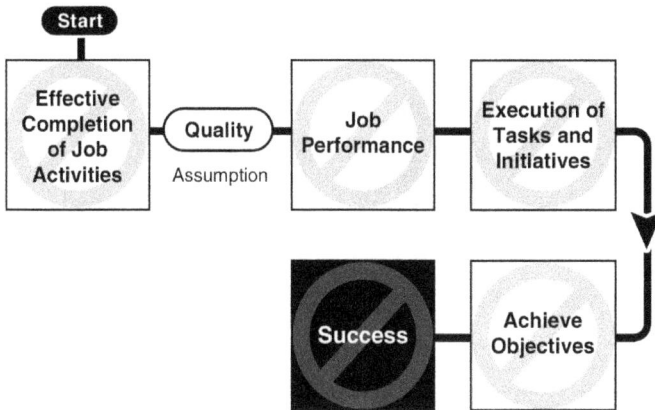

This is the major difference between personal and work goals: if you fall short of accomplishing personal goals, you might rationalize that, even though you may have technically failed, you were still satisfied by the results you attained through the pursuit; it's all subjective.

With work goals, however, you don't have that luxury. Work goals are typically *objective*. This means that your performance is determined by whether or not you achieved the specific and measurable outcomes you were charged with achieving within the given timeframe; either you succeeded or you didn't.

DETERMINANTS OF JOB-RELATED SUCCESS

Your job-success is not determined at the point when you are hired to do a job. Instead, it is determined well before then. Workers' job functions and responsibilities are spelled out based on the things that their organization's leaders have identified as necessary activities that must be performed by the person holding a certain job position if that person is to contribute his or her share to overall organizational success. By successfully performing the identified job functions, the organization's leaders believe that the person holding that specific job will successfully achieve the job-specific objectives necessary for the worker's department, business unit, and ultimately, the organization to achieve *its* objectives, thus contributing to organizational success.

Comprehending this dynamic between a worker's success and his or her contribution to the organization's success requires a general understanding of the strategic planning process through which organizations' and workers' goals and objectives (determinants of success) are defined.

An organization's leaders will define a long-term vision of what they want the organization to be or become in some future, multi-year timeframe. To fulfill its vision, the organization must develop a plan for how it will get there. This plan will consist of shorter-term targets and milestones, referred to as goals and objectives, and a supporting action plan designed to help the organization achieve its defined goals and objectives.

GOALS

A goal is a broad, often-qualitative intended outcome of an initiative or an activity in which the organization is engaged that indicates success or improvement in organizational performance. Goals are the most important things that an organization needs to accomplish if it is to deliver value to its stakeholders, gain a competitive advantage, thrive, or even survive. Examples of organizational goals include:

- To become the #1 software company in America (based on the dollar value of sales);
- To significantly increase employee retention rates;
- To improve the patient experience;
- To achieve a Net Promoter Score of 100;
- To add zero waste to landfills via waste management;
- To increase community engagement and outreach; and
- To provide 10,000 older Americans with food each month.

What is worth noting is that only two of these organizational goals ("To achieve a Net Promoter Score of 100" and "To provide 10,000 older Americans with food each month") are specific, quantifiable, and measurable.

The nature of goals is that they can be specific and measurable or non-specific and subjective; in fact, they usually fall into the latter category. Either way, goals are supported by a set of associated *objectives* that, if achieved, would translate into the accomplishment of the related goal. Put differently, if an organization achieves each of its objectives, then, by default, the organization will have achieved its goals; this assumes that the goal-objective relationship has been properly defined.

OBJECTIVES

An objective supports a goal. It is the clear articulation of the thing(s) that must be achieved to successfully accomplish the associated goal. An objective leaves no room for opinion or interpretation and answers the question: What specific, measurable thing(s) must I achieve so that I will know that I have accomplished my goal? The logic goes as follows: If you successfully achieve the objectives that support a related goal, you will have achieved the goal.

Objectives are needed because goals are often subjective, meaning that it could be unclear whether or not a defined goal was actually accomplished. For instance, if a hospital's goal is "to improve the patient experience," how will the hospital know that it has done so? In such cases, the hospital will define specific and measurable objectives (often multiple per goal) that support the goal and help determine whether or not the goal has been accomplished – by virtue of the fact that the associated objectives have been achieved.

If an organization's goal is "To become the #1 software company in America (in dollar sales)" and last year the #1 software company sold $20 million in software, then the objective supporting the organization's goal would be defined in such a way that, if the objective is achieved, the organization would know it has accomplished its related goal.

In this example, a supporting objective to the organization's goal could be: "Achieve $23 million in software sales by December 31st." Based on this objective, if the organization achieves sales of $23M, it will have achieved its objective and sold $3M more software than the $20 million sold by last year's #1 software company, thus crowning the organization as the new #1 software company in America. Achieving this objective means that the organization accomplished its related goal.

JOB-RELATED WORK OBJECTIVES

Job-related objectives are the set of objectives (or "strategic goals") that are specific to a defined job function, and are designed to ensure that the person holding a specific job function within an organization will have a clear understanding (and roadmap) of the things that person must do to help the organization succeed.

A person with the job title of "Business Analyst," for example, will not only have a list of specific activities the person in that role is expected to perform (such as: analyzing some aspect of the organization's processes, procedures, and organizational structure, etc., to identify problems and determine solutions). However, there will also be a set of specific objectives that anyone holding the Business Analyst job will be charged with achieving over the course of some time period, generally 12 months. The objectives that are defined for the Business Analyst to achieve will comprise a list of those things that the organization's leadership has determined are necessary for the person in that job to deliver for the organization to accomplish its goals and prosper.

Job-related work objectives should contain all the characteristics of organizational objectives and business-unit-level objectives; they should be S.M.A.R.T.:

- **Specific**: An objective should be clearly-defined and specific enough so that it passes what I refer to as the "fifth-grade test." If you wrote down the objective and showed it to a fifth-grader, that fifth-grader should be able to clearly understand what you are trying to accomplish. If s/he cannot, then the objective is likely too complicated or confusing.

- **Measurable**: At the end of the measurement period (usually the end of a calendar or fiscal year) when the worker and his or her manager sits down to discuss how well the worker performed that year, the conversation should be rather straightforward: "Worker, you were charged with reducing the number of product defects to 10 or fewer this year. How many defective products did you produce?" If the worker produced 8 defective products this year, then the worker will have had a good year. If, on the other hand, the worker produced 13 defective products this year, the worker will have had a bad year.

Measurable objectives, among other things, make it easy to determine whether or not the worker responsible for achieving objectives did a good job (achieved the objective) or a not-so-good job (did not achieve the objective).

- **Achievable**: When it comes to actually being able to *do* what is required to achieve the objective, the objective should be realistic; the worker should be capable of fulfilling the necessary requirements to achieve the objective. For example, a young pastry chef is hired by a swanky resort to make fancy desserts for its sophisticated clientele. One of the desserts the pastry chef is charged with making is a *chocolate fondant*, a very complex French cake made mostly from chocolate and butter, with little flour. In the center of the chocolate fondant is hot melted chocolate. This dessert is reminiscent of a molten chocolate cake, whereas – to use an analogy

– the molten chocolate cake is a Ford Focus and the chocolate fondant is a Rolls-Royce Phantom. When it comes time for the young pastry chef to make the complex dessert, a dessert that is a major challenge even for French chefs who specialize in the dessert, he cannot make it because he has had no experience even attempting the dessert. Therefore, the young pastry chef's work objective is not realistically achievable *by him*.

Objectives should be *realistically achievable*. Otherwise, pursuit of the objective could be a futile waste of time and destined for failure. This failure would negatively impact the worker's and the organization's performance. For example, one would not base an organization's survival on a plan with unrealistic odds of success; it would be like basing an organization's revenue objectives on winning the lottery: futile.

- **Relevant**: The objective as defined should be relevant and necessary to contribute to accomplishing the goal with which it is associated. When asking the question: "If I achieve this objective will it get me closer to accomplishing the goal that it supports?" the answer should be an unequivocal "yes." If it is not, then the objective should be reconsidered.

- **Time-Bound**: Since goals are defined as being accomplished within some specific timeframe (even long-term goals), the objectives that support the goal must also be completed within a given timeframe to ensure that the goal – which is based on completed objectives – can be realized within the established timeframe.

THE IMPORTANCE OF JOB-RELATED WORK OBJECTIVES

The general-to-specific tasks, duties, functions, and responsibilities of a worker in a specific job are commonly documented in a *job description*. The job description outlines the details of who – by role – performs a specific type of work, how that work is to be completed, and the frequency and purpose of the work, as it relates to an organization's success.

A worker's manager can use his or her job description as a tool to ensure that the worker is meeting job expectations, supporting the idea that the job description is a resource to be used as a guide for gauging job *performance*.

Performance measures job effectiveness and the efficiency with which the worker's job purpose is fulfilled. And one's job *purpose* is articulated in the worker's job-specific objectives.

Job-specific objectives are important for many reasons:

• They provide a roadmap for how the worker can achieve job success;

• They provide focus to the worker, by serving as a guide and reminder of the most important things the worker can and should accomplish in the course of performing his or her job;

- They define the best ways the worker can contribute to the success of his or her team, department, functional area, business unit, and the overall organization;

- They provide the worker with visibility on how the work s/he performs directly contributes to organizational success. This drives engagement which, according to research by Corporate Executive Board, increases a worker's level of engagement, potentially upping his or her performance rating by 20 percentile points, and reducing his or her departure probability by up to 87%;

- They make the annual performance review between the worker and the worker's manager easier and more efficient. This is because the job-specific objectives defined for the worker are, as the name implies, *objective*, meaning specific and measurable; either you did it or you didn't. Either you performed well this year or you did not;

- They support the development of an Action Plan for the worker. This Plan includes specific objectives, the initiatives necessary to achieve associated objectives, the tasks necessary to deliver the initiatives, and the resources required for the worker to complete tasks;

- They support worker productivity by ensuring the discipline that, for all things that a worker *could* spend his or her time on throughout the course of a day, s/he is focused on getting those things done that get him or her a step closer to achieving objectives. By spending time completing these most important or "priority" items first, workers will waste as little time as possible on activities that do not help the worker achieve his or her objectives. And by reducing and/or eliminating wasted time on non-productive activities, the worker's days become, by definition, more productive;

- They enable workers to gauge their progress toward completing initiatives related to achieving their defined objectives. Task-completion results in finishing up initiatives (or projects) which are, in turn, determined by the worker's job-related objectives. By completing important/priority tasks, the worker will make progress toward finishing related initiatives and bring the worker closer to achieving his or her work objectives – progress that can be measured and tracked;

- They can help the worker manage his or her earnings. Depending on the job, the worker may also be able to manage his or her income. For example, if you are a sales professional or serve in some other position in which part of your compensation is based on completing specific initiatives and objectives, such as, *achieve your sales target of selling $100,000 worth of shoes by the end of the* *year and earn a 5% bonus*; or *exceed your sales target, and for every $10,000 increment above your sales target of $100,000, you will receive an additional 3% bonus,* you have the ability to decide which bonus you will pursue based on what you believe is in your best financial interest. For example, you could decide whether it is more valuable for you financially to spend your time trying to exceed your sales target by $10,000 to earn the extra 3% bonus, or if it's better for you to spend that time trying to achieve one of your other work objectives.

Job success should not be subjective; it should be *objective*. Therefore, the determinants of one's job-related success should be specific, measurable, and clearly defined (i.e., easy to determine what success means for the worker and when success has been achieved).

Measurement is a vehicle used to ascertain the degree to which one's performance meets some desired performance standard. What is implicit in this statement is that one's performance should be based on metrics. Metrics are parameters or measures of quantitative assessment used to track performance. Performance metrics are specific to an organization's purpose and directly related its goals. But mostly, **performance metrics are designed to define and measure success or failure**.

Every organization wants to improve its performance and that of its workers. To upgrade the performance of something, you must be able to measure its existing per-formance level. Measurement requires metrics, and met-rics should be quantitative, otherwise there can be sub-jectivity as to whether or not a performance metric was achieved at a satisfactory level.

Below are two sets of job-success criteria: one set [A] is objective, specific, and measurable, and the other set [B] is subjective, ambiguous, and open to interpretation.

A: Objective Job Success Criteria (Clearly-defined)	B: Subjective Job Success Criteria (Ambiguous)
1. Sign up 500 new subscribers to our newsletter by 12/31/20XX;	1. Increase year-over-year sales within your geographic territory this year;
2. Sell $25,000 in computer maintenance service (at a minimum profit margin of 65%) to companies in Philadelphia. The contracts must be signed by 12/31/20XX;	2. Improve overall customer satisfaction to create more loyal referral customers;
3. Reduce the customer churn rate (the rate of attrition; the percentage of buyers who discontinue their use of a service within a given time period) by 25% compared with last year. To be achieved by 12/31/20XX;	3. Help maintain a positive working environment by serving as resource for other new-hires.
4. Obtain 8 hours of Accounting & Auditing CPE (Continuing Professional Education) credits by 10/31/20XX.	4. Improve employee morale by being the best, most supportive manager you can be.

If, for example, Jill West, a salesperson, was charged with achieving objective A-2 from the table above ("Sell $25,000 in computer maintenance service at a minimum profit margin of 65% to companies in Philadelphia. The contracts must be signed by 12/31/20XX"), Jill would know exactly what she was working toward and she would be able, throughout the year, to gauge her progress toward achieving that objective based on the dollar amount of computer maintenance service contracts she sold each month. Because Jill's job objective is clearly-defined, specific, and measurable, Jill and her manager will have a productive end-of-year performance review discussion. Jill's manager will be able to review Jill's objective of selling $25,000 in computer maintenance service, and determine her success at achieving this objective: did Jill sell $25,000 in maintenance service to companies in Philadelphia by the due date, or not? If the answer is "yes," then Jill will have had a successful year. If the answer is "no," then either the manager will have to probe deeper to identify any extenuating circumstances that may have hampered her ability to achieve the $25,000 sales target, or the manager will determine that Jill simply fell short of achieving the objective and, therefore, will rate her performance accordingly.

On the contrary, if Bob West, a manager, was charged with achieving the subjective work goal B-4 from the table above ("Improve employee morale by being the best, most

supportive manager you can be"), the end-of-year performance evaluation discussion between Bob and his manager would unfold very differently.

To start with, how would Bob be able to realistically
determine whether or not he was actually helping "improve employee morale?" How would he measure it? How
would results be determined at the end of the year? How
could Bob's supervisor conclude that he had successfully
maintained a positive working environment – not to men-
tion the other part of the performance criteria requiring
Bob to be the "most supportive manager you can be?" The
answer is that he wouldn't be able to; therein is the problem.

When Bob and his manager sit down to discuss his
performance over the course of the year, Bob will argue
that, yes, he was able to improve employee morale, and
yes, he was also the most supportive manager he could be.
Therefore, Bob could argue, I should receive an excellent
performance review, because I achieved my objectives.
Bob's manager, on the other hand, could argue the opposite point that, in her *opinion*, no, Bob did not improve
morale, nor was he very supportive to his team. So, the
manager could conclude, based on her *general feel* for the
goings-on within the unit, that Bob fell short of delivering
on the goal, and she would therefore give him an unsatis-
factory performance rating on that goal.

You can guess what happens next: Bob says, "I did,"

and his manager says, "No, you didn't," and they begin to debate the point. Because the performance criteria is ambiguous, there is no way to decide who is right. There is no objective, measurable way to determine whether or not Bob was successful at his job this year (based on that criteria), so, both Bob and his manager would have to rely on their *opinions* to reach a conclusion.

An opinion is a viewpoint based on one's paradigm – how we see the world around us. Opinions are statements that are not conclusive, because they usually involve subjective matters. This dramatically differs from dealing with objective matters (which could be considered facts) which are more likely to be measurable and, therefore, verifiable.

Ambiguity related to such an important matter as one's job performance can understandably lead to a disagreement between parties. This disagreement may ultimately escalate into a conflict.

A "poor" performance rating could cost the worker money (because compensation is often tied to job performance), the opportunity for advancement within his or her organization (because promotions and better job assignments are often tied to job performance), credibility, and even respect. In addition, a poor performance rating could call the worker's job security into question and it could make the worker feel like a failure. All of this decreases the worker's overall level of engagement in his or her job, leading to poor performance and increasing the likelihood of voluntary attrition.

These opposing positions (based on each party's *opinion*, no less) can lead the worker to feel that his or her livelihood is being threatened, which could be perceived as a threat to his or her family's well-being. This is how disagreements over a worker's subjective performance can escalate from disagreement to conflict, creating the potential for heated arguments between the worker and the manager. These arguments – as happens far more often than many people are aware of – can escalate into physical fights or, unfortunately, other forms of violence.

Fortunately, in recent years, organization leaders have begun paying greater attention to the link between clarity of its workers' goals and objectives, and, ultimately, its potential impact on the manager-worker relationship. This awareness has led to organizational development efforts focused on strengthening workers' job performance measures to make them more specific and measurable.

Job-related work objectives should serve several key functions. They should:

- Define those things that are required for a worker in a specific job to successfully achieve for the organization to pursue its mission;

- Define those achievements toward which the worker should strive if s/he is to do his or her part to help the organization succeed;

- Provide a link between the activities the worker performs in the course of doing his or her job, and the impact those activities have on the organization's overall performance and success;
- Dictate the worker's day-to-day activities;
- Clearly and unambiguously define what is required for the worker to have a "successful" year performing his or her job;
- Provide a roadmap for how the worker can grow, develop, and become successful in his or her role or current field or work.

While this list is not exhaustive, it nonetheless provides insight into the importance of clearly-defined, unambiguous, measurable, job-specific work objectives for both the worker and the organization.

The work objectives assigned to an employee's job should be linked with the success of the worker (successfully achieving the objectives defined for his or her role), the worker's department or business unit (the collective success of all workers in a department or business unit should lead to the success of that entity), and the organization as a whole (the success of all departments and business units across the organization should result in the successful accomplishment of an organization's goals – indicators of success).

THE RELATIONSHIP BETWEEN JOB-SUCCESS, BUSINESS UNIT SUCCESS, AND ORGANIZATIONAL SUCCESS

At the highest levels within an organization, the organization's leaders will develop a strategy that defines what they must do to create value for their stakeholders (goals), and how they will create value (objectives). These "whats" and "hows" then cascade through the divisions, departments, business units, and functional areas of the organization, and then serve to inform these entities' priorities. From here, goals and objectives subsequently cascade out to the workers who work in those areas.

When the cascaded goals and objectives arrive at the worker-level – where the *real* work gets done – they are added to the workers' annual performance plans as individual goals and objectives to be achieved if workers are to be considered to have had a successful year. These worker-specific goals and objectives are created such that, when the worker successfully achieves them, that worker's success will contribute to the success of his or her division, department, business unit, or functional area. And when the divisions, departments, business units, and functional areas succeed, as a result of the workers' job-success, the entire organization will succeed.

The Relationship Between Job-Success, Business-Unit Success, and Organizational Success

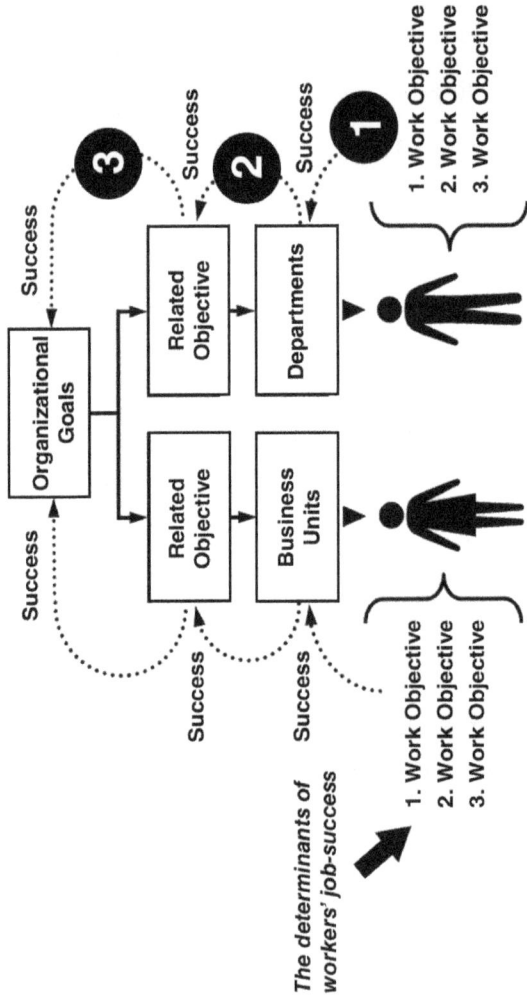

3

CHAPTER TRE

THE BENEFITS OF JOB SUCCESS

If your organization's leaders issued an employee engagement or workplace survey whereby they asked workers, "What are the top 3 benefits of successfully performing your job," they would likely get answers like: (1) I make more money; (2) I get to keep my job; and (3) I will continue to receive health benefits. Depending on the job position the worker holds within the organization, the organization's leaders might hear someone say that an additional benefit of their job success is that they will effectively position themselves for job promotions or career advancement.

If the leaders asked the question differently, such as, "Why do you care if you perform your job *unsuccessfully?*" the responses would be the exact same as the responses to the previous positively-phrased question, but stated from a negative perspective, such as: (1) I won't make more money; (2) I might lose my job; and (3) If I lose my job, I would lose my health benefits. They will also hear some employees respond that they would not set themselves up for a better job, but will, instead, possibly be demoted.

While the responses to these questions will vary, the point remains the same: there is value in doing your job successfully.

It is true that job success usually provides job security, a higher salary and better benefits, and even the opportunity to be promoted into a higher-level job. However, there are other benefits to succeeding in (or even having) a job that, while intrinsically understood by most people in and out of the workforce, would infrequently be provided as an answer to the original question of the top 3 job-success benefits. These would include such things as, the dignity of work, happiness, and self-confidence, to name only a few.

Below are several valuable benefits associated with successfully performing a job; some are quite obvious, whereas others are not.

Pride and Self-Confidence Based on Accomplishment

To accomplish something is to complete the endeavor as it was expected to be completed. A "sense" of accomplishment is that good feeling we get when we complete something of significance as it was intended to be completed, especially if we exceed expectations. When we do, we feel good about ourselves. Let me explain.

In American schools, it is common for teachers to work to make kids feel good about themselves as a way to help them develop "self-esteem."

Self-esteem – whether high or low – is about self-worth. It is the *value* we ascribe to ourselves, how we perceive our value to the world, and how valuable we think we are to others. People with low self-esteem, for example, are more distressed by failure, blame others for their shortcomings, and tend to interpret non-critical comments as critical. On the other hand, people with high self-esteem have an ability to make mistakes and learn from them; they don't place blame at the feet of others, and they use failure as a growth and development opportunity.

The individual with high self-esteem has the ability to accept his or her shortcomings, which is a form of self-acceptance. This individual understands his or her personal strengths and limitations, acknowledge one's imperfections, and has the confidence to make improvements in his or her life.

In his 1943 paper, "A Theory of Human Motivation," psychologist Abraham Maslow introduced his concept of a hierarchy of needs. In this theory, he argued that our physiological needs, security needs, social needs, esteem needs, and self-actualizing needs play a major role in motivating our behavior. According to Maslow, the need for [self-] esteem would intrinsically motivate a student, for example, to earn better grades and to be a better person to satisfy his or her esteem-need.

Given this understanding of the benefits of self-esteem, it is no wonder why parents, coaches, and teachers want to do their part to instill a sense of self-esteem in young kids. This is manifest in such oft-debated ideas as *everybody gets a trophy*, every kid receives a gold star on their homework (even when it is done poorly), and books that reinforce for kids that they are "special" by amplifying their great qualities. The problem with these approaches is that there is no proof that they work for the purpose for which they were intended. These things, it has been argued, only succeed in giving kids a false sense of their skills and talent levels and instill a sense of entitlement. This can be counterproductive and lead kids to not work as hard as they should to *truly* earn that trophy or gold star; why should they? They've always done things "perfectly," as evidenced by the large number of trophies and ribbons they have.

In an article published on the website Psychology Today, Dr. Richard E. Cytowic, a professor of neurology at

George Washington University, writes that "If you want self-esteem, then do estimable things." He argues that accomplishments must be earned through individual effort, and that it is the *endeavor* that generates a sense of pride and esteem.

Doing a job successfully provides workers with a feeling of accomplishment. When a person successfully accomplishes a significant job goal, they not only realize the benefits that accompany successful goal-accomplishment (for example, earning more money or receiving a promotion), but they also gain the motivation to strive to become even better. In doing so, they move closer toward becoming truly fulfilled at work and even, to some degree, in life.

While I do not believe it is productive to base one's self-worth (or even one's value as a worker) on professional achievements, I do believe that accomplishing job-related work goals makes us feel good. And, when we feel good about our work, we are happier and more engaged. And, when we are engaged, we are more productive and more professionally satisfied. Our self-confidence grows based on our ability to accomplish that which we have set out to accomplish, and we feel proud.

Financial and Non-Monetary Incentives

When a worker performs successfully in his or her job, there is an opportunity to earn more money. Duh!

However, depending on the specific organization and a worker's job within it, successfully performing a job can provide other monetary incentives beyond simply a pay-raise. These incentives may include: bonuses, commission accelerators, stock and stock options, profit-sharing, and even paid-time-off to attend award trips, such as The President's Club celebration, for example.

In addition to monetary incentives, organizations often reward successful workers with non-monetary-yet-valuable perks, such as higher-level training (especially if the worker's performance has identified him or her as a HiPo - high potential employee), flexible work hours, and/or a coveted parking spot.

Recognition

Workplace experts often share that, when asked, workers say they value recognition of a "job well done" more than they do money; I'm throwing the flag on that one, for no other reason than it is somewhat counter to my actual experiences of managing large teams of people. But, I do agree that workers who receive recognition for successful job performance and other significant accomplishments have improved morale and a better attitude within the workplace.

Recognition incentives can include almost anything that lets the workers know that their accomplishments and efforts have not gone unnoticed and are much appreciated. Common forms of recognition include: a direct "thank you" from senior-level managers, public announcements regarding the worker's accomplishments, positive added responsibilities (such as mentoring others on how to achieve similar success), dinner for two, and the usual plaques, certificates of recognition, coffee mugs, and other trinkets.

Ultimately, as with money, it is not the prize itself that provides value to the worker. Instead, it is the fact that his or her efforts have been noticed and appreciated.

The Value of Work Itself, Continued Employment

Having a job, or "work," is not simply exchanging labor for wages. Work is beneficial to health and well-being, and it provides us with a sense of self-worth and dignity; it gives meaning to a worker's personal life.

As sociologist Dominique Schnapper at The Center for Social Studies of the University of Coimbra explains:

> Deprived from his/her space and time references, the unemployed person feels like he/she has lost his/her dignity. He/she lives through a personal identity crisis that jeopardizes both family roles and relationships in general. Isolation and de-socialization are integral to what we may call 'the unemployment test.'

Work plays an important role in structuring an employee's daily life and protects against boredom and emptiness. It helps workers form both personal and social identity; it helps create relationships and lifelong bonds; it provides a daily routine and a level of physical and mental activity. It contributes to our well-being and it makes us feel as though we are contributing to our community and are a part of society; it gives us a sense of self-esteem, pride, and self-worth.

There is evidence showing that joblessness is associated with poorer mental and physical health compared with being gainfully-employed. Work can reverse the adverse effects of unemployment as Cary L. Cooper and Alexander-Stamatios G. Antoniou detail in their book *The Psychology of the Recession on the Workplace*.

In the book, *Is Work Good for Your Health and Well-being?*, Gordon Waddell and A. Kim Burton conclude that: work is beneficial to health and well-being; lack of work is detrimental to health and well-being. For unemployed individuals, re-employment generates improvements in health and well-being; and continued unemployment leads to further deterioration.

It's no secret that some percentage of workers in all organizations, across all industries, around the world, will hate their jobs; it is simply inevitable. However, for the reasons described above, I believe it is important for even disgruntled workers to appreciate the value of work itself, and, before abandoning a job or becoming so disengaged that their work output suffers and their voluntary departure no longer becomes an option that they control, figure out ways to become more engaged in their jobs and/or their workplaces.

Happiness

When we get something we want, such as successfully accomplishing a significant goal that we set out to accomplish, our brain releases dopamine. This chemical is often known as the "feel good" neurotransmitter because it does just that – it makes us feel good. When we feel good, we are generally happier; success breeds joyful happiness.

In his book *Flourish: A Visionary New Understanding of Happiness and Well-being*, Martin Seligman argues that genuine well-being comes from promoting five elements of well-being: pleasure, engagement, relationships, meaning, achievement – these five elements are also known as P.E.R.M.A.

Pleasure is, simply put, feeling good. *Engagement* is associated with having a good, full life comprised of satisfying work, close relationships with family and friends, and interesting hobbies. *Meaning* refers to feeling part of a larger purpose. *Meaning* and *achievement* are consistent with Maslow's need for *self-actualization*. While all elements of well-being are important, they are not equally important. Seligman believes *engagement* and *meaning* are most crucial for achieving a happy life.

Perhaps the most important aspect of happiness is how it tangibly benefits people. Studies by psychologist Ed Diener, one of the most well-respected researchers in the field of positive psychology, found compelling evidence that happiness improves physical health and lengthens lives. The evidence is so compelling that some research suggests overall health and well-being can be significantly impacted simply by being happy.

The benefits of job success go well beyond just earning more money, keeping your job, and getting a promotion. Job success breeds confidence, a feeling of self-worth, pride, a sense of belonging, well-being, health, and happiness. These benefits of "a job well done" should motivate all workers to strive to do their jobs successfully. Doing one's job successfully doesn't start on your first day on the job. It starts even before you are hired for that job.

4

CHAPTER **FOUR**

THE ANATOMY OF JOB SUCCESS

On a macro level, a worker's job success is dictated by goals and objectives defined for the worker by organizational leadership. On a more micro level, however, a worker's job success is a function of several factors, including: the goodness of fit between the worker's skills and the requirements for the job to which s/he has been assigned; the availability and accessibility of internal support and training; the worker's level of engagement; the degree of alignment between organizational goals and the worker's individual performance plan; and eventually, the quality of goals and the objective defined for the worker in the individual performance plan.

JOB-FIT

Job success – a worker's ability to achieve job-specific objectives defined by the organization's leadership – can be traced back to the point at which the worker-as-job applicant decides to apply for a specific job at a specific company.

The job-seeker, whom we will call "Bob," believes that he possesses exchange-value in the form of his human capital. He believes he can exchange this with an organization for something of equal value, like a job that pays money.

"Human Capital" is not simply an organization's employee. Rather, it is the proficiency, value, or capital that the (human) employee brings to her or his job, resulting in a return for the organization.

In some literature, human capital is synonymous with "employee" or "worker" or some other description of an organization's human resources. In practice, however, human capital is more a collective of *attributes* that an employee or worker possesses, including:

- The worker's ability;
- The worker's qualifications and knowledge (acquired via formal education);
- The worker's skills, competency, and expertise (acquired through on-the-job training); and
- The worker's motivation and level of engagement.

Within organizations, people and their human capital drive strategy execution. Therefore, organizations that wish to give themselves the best chance of being successful (as determined by accomplishing goals and objectives defined in their strategy) must develop a *human capital strategy* to ensure that the necessary proficiencies are appropriately brought to bear by the right people in the right quantities in the right roles, thereby increasing the likelihood that the organization's strategies will be successfully executed.

In most organizations, certain job functions require a degree of proficiency and ability that may not be immediately available in its current employee population. When this occurs, organizations will post job openings in the hopes of attracting qualified candidates who can successfully perform the duties and responsibilities of the posted position.

Job postings normally contain a job description which provides useful information about the open position to prospective job applicants. These descriptions also include the duties, responsibilities, and necessary qualifications for job. From this information, job-seekers, like Bob, can determine whether or not they are interested in the job and, more importantly, whether they meet the qualifications for the position and possess the requisite skills and experience to actually *do* the job.

So, if Bob is interested in the job based on what he has

read about it, and if he believes that he has the skills and experience needed to successfully perform the job duties, then he will apply as a job candidate; he will submit his resume and an application.

Upon receiving Bob's job application, the job recruiter at the organization to which Bob has applied for the job will compare Bob's credentials and experience against the job requirements. If the recruiter believes that there is a fit between Bob's job interests and background, and the needs of the hiring organization, the recruiter will schedule an interview to discuss the job with Bob and get a better sense of whether or not he or she believes that Bob is a candidate worth considering. At the same time, Bob can gain further insight into the organization and the position to help him decide whether or not he believes there is a good fit between his work interests and the job to which he applied.

After the initial interview, the recruiter will make a determination on whether or not s/he believes that Bob is a worthy candidate for the position and warrants a second in-person interview. After all the interviews and conversations have been completed, assuming Bob is still interested in the job, the recruiter will decide whether or not to extend Bob a job offer based on the recruiter's assessment of whether Bob is capable of successfully performing the job.

The job-fit between a worker's skills, knowledge, experience, and ability, the duties and responsibilities of the job for which she or he is being considered, and the needs of the hiring organization is **the first stage in the anatomy of a worker's job success**.

JOB-FIT GAPS

Continuing with the above-mentioned example, if the job recruiter believes that Bob's skills and experience align with the duties and responsibilities of the open job, the recruiter will offer him the job. And if Bob accepts the job offer, then he will officially become a worker in the hiring organization. It is at this point where the first influences on job success manifest themselves.

The goodness-of-fit between the requirements of the job and Bob's ability to perform the job requirements will reveal gaps if Bob is unable to effectively perform all the major job duties. A job-fit gap is revealed when it is discovered that a new-hire, like Bob, cannot actually perform all the job requirements. The more job-fit gaps that exist between the worker and the job he was hired to do, the lower the odds that the worker will be successful at the job. For example, if the job required ten significant activities to be performed, and Bob could only successfully perform seven of the activities, then, simplistically, Bob would have a 70% chance at succeeding in the job.

From an overall organizational perspective, taking all its workers into consideration, any mismatch or "gap" between the talent required to perform a job effectively and the talent available reduces the organization's likelihood of executing its strategy, accomplishing its desired goals, and improving its performance.

If the organization in the above example is unable to get Bob the training and coaching he needs to close the gaps and perform all the duties for which he was hired, then it is unlikely that Bob will be successful in the job.

The Harvard Business Review states that up to 80% of employee turnover is due to bad hiring decisions. When it comes to hiring job candidates from outside the hiring organization, people have a bad track record when it comes to identifying successful job candidates. The Society for Human Resource Management (SHRM) reports that, on average, 36% of new hires fail within the first 18 months and 40% of senior managers hired from outside the organization fail within 18 months of being brought on board.

The reasons why new-hires fail at such surprising rates can be manifold, but it is often the result of the improper gathering and analysis of applicant-related information. The data available and the assumptions made about the job candidate based on the prospective worker's application data, resume, and interviews play a key role in the success or failure of selecting good employees.

INTERNAL SUPPORT AND TRAINING

Job-fit gaps – the disconnect between a worker's skills and ability, and the job duties to which s/he has been assigned – are common within organizations; after all, nobody's perfect. What job recruiters hope for in a candidate, however, is the ability to perform *most* of the primary job requirements and the ability to learn or acquire the skills necessary to perform an even higher percentage of the job requirements over time. This requires the organization to make an "investment" in the worker.

In most organizations, certain job functions require a degree of proficiency and ability that may not be immediately available in its employee population. These organizations, however, believe that they do have workers who – with additional education, training, and development – can become a perfect fit to fill the jobs in question. In these cases, the organization's leaders may make the decision to invest in the workers' human capital to achieve that end.

When organizations invest in a worker, they are investing in the worker's *human capital* (the worker's ability, qualifications and knowledge, skill, competency, and expertise, as well as their motivation and level of engagement) to upgrade the worker's job performance, close the gaps, and contribute to organizational success. Just like with any other *capital investment* an organization makes, the organization expects a return on investment in the form of performance improvements leading to the successful achievement of goals and objectives, thereby contributing to overall organizational success.

Many variables can affect the performance of workers in the workplace. These variables can include an employee's level of engagement, working hours, training and development opportunities, stress, recognition and rewards, and culture, to name a few. Some of these variables are outside the control of the worker and some do not directly determine one's performance level. There are variables, however, that are both under the worker's control *and* are performance determinants.

Organizational psychologist John P. Campbell developed a hierarchical model of job performance based on extensive research. Campbell advanced three direct Determinants of Job Performance that focus on variables directly under the individual's control:

- **Declarative Knowledge**: Understanding what is required to perform a task.

- **Procedural Knowledge**: Knowing how to perform a job or task.

- **Motivation**: The intrinsic choice to perform at a high level – putting forth one's best effort. This is consistent with the employee engagement concept.

There is an additional determinant that, while not specifically defined as one of Campbell's determinants, is nonetheless an important determinant of one's job performance, and that is *Problem Solving*. This is the process of completing a task or reaching a goal when the means for reaching that goal have not yet been identified.

An investment in human capital for the purpose of improving employee job performance should be targeted at those levers that positively impact and upgrade performance by affecting the primary performance determinants. Investing in education, training, and the opportunity for workers to gain relevant experience has been shown to positively improve performance by increasing declarative knowledge and/or procedural knowledge. In addition, financial and "recognition" rewards (investments) have also been shown to positively impact performance by increasing motivation and engagement.

It is not enough, however, for an organization to simply make these investments *available* to workers. Workers must have *access* to these investment vehicles and, quite often, these improvement initiatives must be *required* of the worker by, for instance, including them in the worker's performance plan as a growth and development opportunity.

The inability or failure of an organization to provide and make available such investments can negatively impact the worker's job success by leaving unfilled job-gaps, thus reducing the worker's chances of performing his or her job as effectively as necessary.

WORKER ENGAGEMENT

Many organizations adopt employee attraction, retention, and engagement strategies, because *all* organizations want their workers to be fully engaged at work. Engaged workers intrinsically strive to do a good job for the sake of doing a good job, not necessarily because they are coerced or cajoled into doing so. Engaged workers also voluntarily remain with their organizations longer than workers who are not fully engaged, thus reducing work discontinuity and voluntary-attrition costs.

Frequent voluntary turnover has a negative impact on employee morale, productivity, and an organization's revenue. In addition, recruiting and training a new employee requires time and money, sometimes as much as 60% more money than the cost of retaining an existing employee.

The Center for American Progress reports that for workers earning less than $50,000 annually – which covers three-quarters of all workers in the United States – the typical cost of turnover is 20% of the employee's salary. So, if a departing employee had an annual salary of $50,000, the cost to replace that employee would be approximately $10,000. Multiply that figure by the number of employees who voluntarily leave an organization each year (a 2013 CompData Surveys report found that the average voluntary employee turnover rate in all industries in the U.S. was 10.4%), and you can gain an appreciation for the importance of employee retention.

Engagement is about commitment on the part of the worker, whether the commitment is rational (driven by the benefits the worker receives for doing the job, such as income, health benefits, training and development, good relationships, and others) or emotional (they see value in their work, they enjoy their job).

The Corporate Leadership Council (CLC), in its comprehensive study entitled *Driving Employee Performance and Retention Through Engagement*, has identified 160 broadly applied levers that build general workforce engagement. These are organized into eight categories:

- Qualities of the Direct Manager;
- Qualities of the Senior Executive Team;
- Compensation Plans;
- Benefit Plans;
- Onboarding;
- Day-to-Day Work;
- Learning and Development;
- Organizational Culture.

The more levers that the organization is deficient at, the lower the potential for its workers to be fully engaged at work. Take the "Qualities of the Direct Manager" lever, for example, which includes such levers defined by the CLC as:

- Commitment to Diversity;
- Demonstrates Honesty and Integrity;
- Adapts to Changing Circumstances;
- Clearly Articulates Organizational Goals;
- Possesses Job Skills; and
- Sets Realistic Performance Expectations.

This set of manager-controlled levers or *qualities* directly impacts a worker's motivation, effort, performance, commitment, and willingness to stay at the organization for which s/he works.

There is an old saying that "People don't quit a job, they quit a boss." While this might not always be the reason why workers voluntarily leave a job, people are, in fact, more likely to quit a job if they have a horrible boss.

A 2015 Gallup study found that roughly 50% of the 7,200 adults surveyed said they had left a job "to get away from their manager." Interestingly, more than half of the survey respondents gave the "highest agreement rating" to the statement, "I feel I can approach my manager with any type of question." These workers are considered actively engaged in their work, which, according to *The Wall Street Journal*, suggests that manager openness may relate to engagement and worker productivity. A good proxy for the strength of the worker-manager relationship is the comfort level an employee has with approaching his or her manager with any type of question. This comfort is influenced by the above-mentioned list of manager qualities.

If the manager does not provide coaching, direction, leadership, decision-making, guidance, and apply direct manager levers to the worker-manager relationship, a worker who might be experiencing job-gaps will find it challenging to perform optimally and achieve his or her job objectives.

ALIGNMENT BETWEEN ORGANIZATIONAL GOALS AND THE WORKER'S INDIVIDUAL PERFORMANCE PLAN

Alignment between an organization's goals and the worker's job goals simply means that the organization has cascaded or pushed its goals down throughout each part of the organization – ultimately down to each worker in the organization – and assigned each layer and person in the organization a share of the organization's goals to accomplish. By each part of the organization accomplishing their share of the organization's overall goal, when rolled together, the organization will have successfully accomplished its overall goal.

Alignment is achieved when the organization divides its goals and pushes them down throughout the parts of the organization, including to its workers. When this cascading occurs, each part of the organization and their workers are working on a part of the whole to fulfill a common mission. Alignment is about everyone being on the same page and working toward a common goal.

Suppose, for example, that I started a business called Tab's Donut Shop and I hired two workers, Bob and Ann. To be successful, the donut shop must sell $150,000 in chocolate donuts by the end of the calendar year. To ensure that I sell the requisite amount of chocolate donuts, I cascade (push or allocate) equal parts of that sales goal down to Bob and Ann, such that Bob and Ann are each required to sell $50,000 in chocolate donuts (just as I am). And, if we each accomplish our individual sales goals of $50,000 in chocolate donuts, for a total of $150,000, the company will be successful.

By cascading parts of the overall goal down to Bob and Ann and tying their job performance and bonus to their successfully selling $50,000 in chocolate donuts each, I am driving alignment throughout the company by ensuring that we are all focused on accomplishing the same thing: selling chocolate donuts. As this example illustrated, alignment drives a common focus to accomplish a shared goal. By including the $50,000 sales goal in their performance plans, each of the employees knows what is expected of them and how their performance will be measured. They can also clearly see how their efforts contribute to the success of the donut shop.

A *performance plan* is part of an organization's performance management process, which can include anything from the expectations of a worker's exhibited behavior to the results that are expected to be achieved by the worker in his or her job. For this discussion, I will focus on the latter.

A "job" is a set of related tasks, responsibilities, and actions to be undertaken by a worker to achieve some desired end. A worker's job performance ultimately relates to observable behavior that supports the accomplishment of specific goals and the achievement of defined objectives; it is what a worker is hired to *do*. What a worker is hired to do should be the result of the organization's strategic plan or *strategy*.

The strategy serves as the blueprint that defines what success means to an organization and how that success will be achieved. And the most important aspect of a strategy is its execution – doing the things necessary to bring the organization's goals and mission to fruition. A failed strategy can contribute to an organization's inability to achieve its mission.

The primary reason why strategies fail is poor execution. There is evidence to suggest that improving strategy execution – both in terms of speed and quality – significantly increases the chances of implementing a successful strategy. A key to strategic execution-speed is the organization's workers and how they are mobilized, supported, held accountable, and engaged in organizational strategies. If a strategy is to be given the best chance of success, organizations must develop an approach to cascade organizational goals all the way down to the worker level. And when organizations cascade or distribute each worker's *share* of the organization's overall goals to the worker based on his or her job function, the worker's share of the organization's goals are provided in the worker's job performance plan as individual, measurable goals and objectives (metrics) to be accomplished or achieved by the worker, if the worker is to be considered "successful" in his or her job.

Requiring the execution of goal and objective metrics defined in the worker's performance plan – if that worker is to be deemed successful in his or her job – therefore becomes the organization's most effective way to emphasize the importance of the worker's contribution to overall organizational success.

Goal-Performance Plan Alignment

An organization's workers are more engaged and productive when they know what is expected of them and have a clear understanding of how their role in the organization contributes to the organization's performance, as measured by goal accomplishment.

The performance plan should not simply be a vehicle used to measure job effectiveness and success, it should also be a motivational tool, a development tool, and equally importantly, a guide-rail toward success; it should direct workers' focus toward performing activities and completing tasks that directly contribute to the achievement of their job goals and objectives. By focusing their efforts on those activities that have an impact, workers perform their jobs more productively, increasing the likelihood of their job success.

When there is uncertainty about expectations, priorities, and the determinants of success, workers often end up performing trivial busy work. These workers underperform because they are not clear about exactly what they should be doing or why. When this occurs, they become less engaged at work, which can contribute to poor or unsuccessful job performance.

CLEARLY-DEFINED, SPECIFIC, AND MEASURABLE JOB-RELATED WORK OBJECTIVES

The following is an actual job-related work objective that was included in the performance plan of a previous job that I held:

> **Business Objective:** Ensure readiness for a smooth [technology project] launch and deployment - in particular, for Sales and Customer Maintenance.
> **Start Date:** 00/00/20XX
> **Due Date:** 00/00/20XX
> **Status:** Completed
> **Weight:** 10.0%

The business "objective," as defined, raises several questions: How will my manager or I know whether or not I have actually achieved this objective? How will its achievement be measured (that, was never discussed)? What does "ensure readiness" truly mean? How will we know that readiness has been ensured? What is considered a "smooth launch and deployment" (this was never discussed, either)? What will be considered "smooth;" 5 hiccups or fewer? Success will be based on whose definition or opinion?

When you think about the business objective in this light, it is easy to see that this is actually a business *(un) objective*: a desired outcome that those who crafted it thought was specific and measurable, but is, in reality, not.

As you can imagine, when it came time for the end-of-year performance review between my manager and me, it was more of a *debate* about "did I or didn't I," rather than a discussion.

SEVERAL YEARS AGO, while leading a multi-billion dollar organization, I had a manager on my team ("Phil") who reported directly to me. Subsequently, Phil moved into a different role and, as a result, had a different manager to whom he reported. While he was part of my team, Phil and I developed a great professional working relationship based on trust and openness.

One day during the end-of-year employee performance review period, Phil came into my office to share an incident that had occurred during his performance review with his new manager. Phil's performance plan contained several ambiguous, subjective "objectives" that Phil had been charged with achieving that year. One of the "Business Objectives/Goals for the current period" – the one that ultimately led Phil to my office – was stated in the following way:

> Establish an efficient routine for managing and supporting the needs of the [team]. Seek opportunities to establish goals, metrics, and track performance of the [business unit] function.

As Phil relayed the story, this was the first objective that was discussed. The new manager had not previously known Phil, nor was he fully aware of Phil's reputation as a first-rate employee. The manager began the conversation by asking:

Manager (M): So, Phil, how do you think you did on this business objective this year?

Phil (P): I think I've had a very good year, and I did particularly well on this specific business objective.

M: Why do you say that?

P: Well, as the objective states, I established an efficient routine for managing and supporting the needs of the team and I found opportunities to establish goals and metrics. And I even created a way to track [business unit] performance.

M: Well, if you did in fact do those things, I haven't seen it to the degree that you just described. So, I'm not sure that you did as great a job with these requirements as you just implied.

P: Well, if we dissect the business objective, the first requirement was to "Establish an efficient routine …" I established one. The next requirement was to "Seek opportunities to establish goals, metrics, and track performance …" I sought and uncovered multiple opportunities to do these things. Therefore, according to the specified objective, I did *everything* that I was asked to do! And if I satisfied *all* the requirements as written, then that means I successfully performed this business objective.

M: Well, I don't see it that way, and this conversation is going *nowhere*. Maybe we should get HR involved.

The heated conversation (debate?) continued, but went nowhere.

This story illustrates the major challenges with ambiguous, poorly-defined job-related work objectives:

1. It was open to debate whether or not the worker successfully achieved the objective. In such situations, the worker's job success rests on the often-divergent opinions of both the worker and the manager. Eventually, the manager will "win" this debate (due to his or her authority) and the worker will have to live with these consequences. This could be especially harmful and demotivating if the manager's *opinion* of the worker's performance is unfavorable to the worker.

2. Because of the non-specificity of objectives, the worker will not be able to determine those tasks or job activities in which s/he should engage in to achieve the objectives. This often results in the worker simply performing many action items that will waste his or her time; this is inevitable. And when the worker wastes time performing *non-impactful* activities – activities that, when performed, do not get the worker closer to achieving his or her objectives – the worker becomes unproductive. Unproductive workers perform at a level beneath their capabilities, which ultimately leads to lower job success, worker dissatisfaction, and lower engagement.

3. Poorly-defined objectives result in workers performing job activities that are not directed toward the successful achievement of their job-related work objectives. This happens because workers are not quite sure what will

lead to the successful achievement of these *fuzzy* objectives. When their efforts do not lead to the successful achievement of their job-specific objectives, the worker becomes ineffective at doing his or her part to help the organization succeed. If this scenario is extrapolated across all the organization's workers, then it becomes less likely that the organization will succeed at realizing its goals.

4. Performance plan debates, such as those between Phil and his new manager, can drive a wedge between the worker and manager. As detailed previously, the "Qualities of the Direct Manager" very significantly impact a worker's willingness to stay at his or her current employer, especially such manager levers as *clearly-defined objectives* and a *worker's relationship with the manager*. Remember: A good proxy for the strength of the worker-manager relationship is how comfortable a worker is in approaching the manager with any type of question; manager openness may directly relate to engagement and worker productivity.

5. If a manager is – for whatever reason – "out to get" a worker, then the unscrupulous manager could use the ambiguousness of performance plan objectives to build a case that the worker is a poor performer, making it easier for the manager to jettison the worker from the job or the organization. In such cases, a worker's job

performance becomes a popularity contest, a likeability endeavor, a "featherbedding" (filling your team or organization with "your" people) result, or simply put, an homage to the person who can kiss the most butt.

The less clearly-defined, specific, and measurable a worker's job-related goals and objectives, the greater the likelihood that the worker will be unsuccessful in his or her job.

Putting these anatomical contributors to job-success together, it becomes easier to appreciate how a worker's job-success begins before the worker is hired and carries through a review of how the worker actually performs in the job, based on the achievement of job-related goals and objectives.

The Anatomy of Job-Success

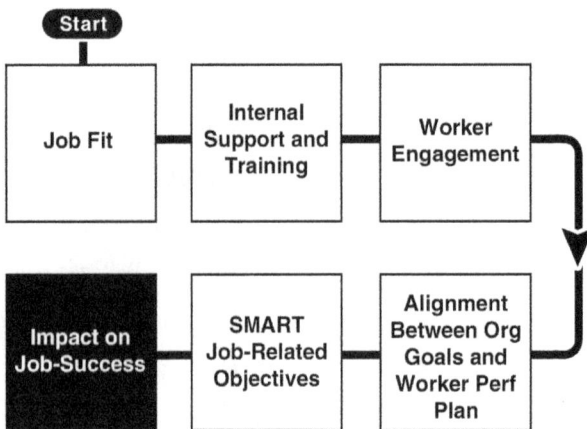

Start

| Job Fit | Internal Support and Training | Worker Engagement |

| Impact on Job-Success | SMART Job-Related Objectives | Alignment Between Org Goals and Worker Perf Plan |

5

WHY WORKERS FAIL [DO NOT SUCCEED]
IN THEIR JOB

While *Chapter 4: The Anatomy of Job Success* provides an understanding of the work-related and organizational factors that can impact a worker's job success, it also serves as a vehicle for understanding why workers fail or do not succeed in their jobs.

I suspect that if you polled 10,000 Human Resources professionals, supervisors, managers, workplace consultants, and others who have had to go through the unfortunate experience of either separating a worker from the organization or studying workplace job separations, you will get at least 5,000 different reasons why one worker or another has been unsuccessful in his or her job.

As a person who has studied workplace performance, worked with organizations on worker job success, *and* has had the unfortunate experience of separating workers from a job based on poor performance, I have identified eight general reasons why workers do not succeed in their jobs.

Identifying the reasons why workers succeed in their jobs, in addition to the reasons why they don't succeed, can serve as a prescription for achieving job success.

REASONS WHY WORKERS FAIL IN THEIR JOBS

REASON #1: JOB-FIT

A poor match between the job requirements and the worker's skills, ability, and experience

As previously shared, it is estimated that up to 80% of employee turnover is due to bad hiring decisions. One of the major contributors to these bad decisions is hiring a person into a job for which they are unqualified. A *qualified* worker is one whose abilities align with the requirements needed to satisfactorily perform a specific job and the associated set of responsibilities.

Job qualification can be many things. However, when we say that someone is not qualified for a job, we typically mean that the person lacks three characteristics that should reveal themselves during the job-candidate-consideration process if the job-fit mistake is to be avoided: the candidate's relevant prior experience; the candidate's current skill level; and the candidate's ability to learn and acquire those capabilities that would close the job-fit gap and bring the candidate up to the desired job proficiency level.

Relevant experience implies that the candidate has previously performed the same or equivalent types of duties that are required to be successful in the job for which the candidate is being considered. If you are applying to become an Executive Administrator, for example, it's a good idea to have had experience acting as an interface and point of contact between executives, internal and external clients, and stakeholders, as well as experience managing the schedules and calendars of multiple people.

One major contributor to hiring candidates with insufficient relevant experience is that recruiters and hiring-managers do not do enough to validate that the experience the candidate has acquired is (1) valid, as stated, and (2) is the right kind of experience. For example, an Executive Administrator job candidate might state on his or her resume that they "have lots of experience scheduling appointments for executives and managing calendars."

However, when the recruiter and manager probe more deeply, they learn that the candidate gained that experience back in 1985 when calendars were paper-based and not electronic, such as the Microsoft, Mozilla, and Google calendars.

A worker's *skill level* is simply the ability to do something "well." For example, a welder might have the skill to clamp broken metal pieces together and melt and apply solder along the adjoining edges of work pieces. A marketing professional might have incredible skills as a storyteller, creating emotionally-compelling stories while using brand-driven storytelling approaches. A police officer might have the ability and skills to calm escalating situations, or negotiate, or even gain trust in the communities s/he serves.

Far too often, organizations will hire workers without ever having tested or ascertained the worker's relevant experience or requisite skills for the job for which they are being considered. An analyst might be quite skilled at structuring databases, but does s/he possess critical-thinking skills or the ability to interpret numbers? How would a recruiter know? How could they test this skill?

Ability means that a person possesses the means or skill to *do* something. It can encompass knowledge, aptitude (such as, the ability to learn new things), and the wherewithal to acquire and apply knowledge and skills.

Ability is the very important aspect of ensuring a fit

between a job candidate's capacity and the requirements to be successful in a job. I say it is important because if a candidate has the relevant experience for a job, but his or her skills in some important aspect of the job is only 80%, if the candidate has the aptitude and ability to learn the other 20% of the job requirements at which s/he is currently deficient, then that candidate can grow into the position, and, eventually, be able to successfully perform the job.

Far too often, recruiters and hiring-managers say, "S/he can do 80% of the things that are required for the person in this job to be successful. Close enough." And they hire the candidate without thinking about whether or not the candidate is capable of learning and applying the other 20% of the job requirements. Ultimately, the worker's performance suffers due to his or her inability to fulfill all the job requirements.

REASON #2: WORKER DEVELOPMENT

A lack of internal support and training

It is no sin to hire an on-paper-impressive job candidate even though that candidate does not possess 100% of the skills or knowledge that are stipulated for the position; in fact, this happens about 90% of the time when organizations hire new employees. The problem arises when the worker is fully entrenched in the job and it becomes evident that, for the worker to perform his or her job to the expected degree, the worker will need further training and development, but the organization does not provide the training necessary to bring the worker's performance up to the necessary level necessary for job success. "Sure, the candidate for the accounting job is proficient with data analytics, advanced modeling techniques, and SQL (a programming language)," the recruiter says, "but s/he does not possess general business knowledge. Oh well, maybe s/he can pick it up once he or she is in the position."

However, frequently the organization does not provide the training necessary for the worker to acquire that business knowledge. As a result, the worker never fully develops into the job. He or she will likely not perform successfully, and may never become fully engaged in the role or within the organization. This is consistent with a survey that finds that 74% of workers felt they were not achieving their full potential at work.

According to the GO2 Tourism HR Society, a recent survey indicates that 40% of employees who receive poor job training leave their positions within the first year. These employees cite the lack of skills training and development as the principal reason for moving on.

While it is encouraging that the training spend by organizations has increased about 25% since 2008, a counterbalancing reality is that 70% of on-the-job learning occurs informally, research shows. I believe that any channel – even informal ones – through which a worker can learn things to help him or her perform better in their job is a good thing. However, informal learning should become more formalized if it is to have the greatest adoption and impact on organizational goals.

Training helps workers develop usable skills that will help them contribute more effectively to the organization. As workers learn new skills, perform better in their jobs due to improved skills, and contribute to the organization to a greater degree, they become more engaged. Training promotes job satisfaction.

Many years ago, when I was a young salesman at the IBM Corporation, workers worked from the office to a greater degree than we do today. One of the benefits this afforded was the ability to learn from more experienced sales pros every day; this helped us become better sales professionals.

As Michael Maupin, author of the book *The Billion Dollar Deal* puts it: "Back in those days, we interacted each and every day with seasoned, successful senior salespeople. They would take us out on sales calls with them to let us see how it's done, they would help us with our sales strategies, they would help us understand the sales process, and they would help us to separate sales fact from sales fiction."

Today, many organizations have moved to teleworking and hoteling office models in which people work remotely (e.g. from a home office) and there are no assigned desks in the office, so visitors can sit anywhere. Because of this arrangement, young workers in many industries lose the benefit of learning the ropes from more senior workers, since young and new workers infrequently get to interact in a meaningful way with more seasoned workers. This is one reason why training has become essential for knowledge transfer. It is especially important if only a few workers possess special skills; you'll have a tough time recouping their knowledge if they suddenly leave the company. Thus, it becomes even more important for there to be a way to share their knowledge with others in the organization. Training is one way for organizations to address these issues.

Formal training is not the only vehicle that provides workers with the knowledge and development necessary to be successful in their jobs. An organization's internal support structure can also help workers bridge the job-gap.

Internal support structures can take many forms, including managers, mentors (both formal and informal); work teams; "Buddies;" organization-supported external groups; and "Buffalo" arrangements – a term we coined several years ago at The Water Group to describe a formal arrangement via which organizations will pair senior workers with junior and new employees on projects as a way for the junior/new workers to learn and benefit from the value of the senior workers' experience.

If job-gaps exist with workers and there is no formal or informal mechanism in place to help the worker close the gap, then a worker's chance of being successful in their jobs decreases dramatically.

REASON #3: WORKER ENGAGEMENT

Uncommitted workers do not give their full effort

As discussed previously, workers' level of engagement (how committed they are to their work, the company, and how much effort they put forth in the name of doing a good job) can be impacted by many things, such as their relationship with their managers.

Given the time, money, effort, heartaches, and headaches that often accompany the firing and hiring process, it stands to reason that, once an organization has made the decision to hire a new worker, the organization should expend similar effort in keeping the upstanding worker in the fold. In addition, organizations should also invest in a worker's ongoing development to support their ability to perform as productively as possible and to be successful in their job.

Simplistically, workers are more inclined to remain with an organization when they are "rationally" committed to the organization. Rational commitment is driven by factors such as a living wage (income), health benefits, paid time off (vacation days), and a comfortable working environment – however, "comfort" is defined by the worker. Until an organization satisfies these basic requirements for most workers, the organization will find it challenging to get a worker to commit to staying with the organization.

In "A Theory of Human Motivation," Abraham Maslow argued that all human behavior is motivated by need, and he defined a hierarchy of needs, explaining that until one's basic, lower-level needs are met (such as the need for food, water, and shelter – physiological needs) a person would not be concerned with satisfying higher-level needs, such as the need to achieve job success, for example. Until lower-level needs are met, workers cannot perform optimally, if at all.

Maslow's idea of lower-level needs, like physiological and safety needs, are consistent with the things that are required for a worker to be rationally-committed to a job or an organization. If job rewards are sufficiently provided for, workers will be more inclined to want to stay at a job.

A worker is said to be *emotionally*-committed to a job when they derive pride, enjoyment, inspiration, or excitement from a job. These things drive workers to want to give their best effort to the job and the organization, often leading to improved performance by the worker and greater success.

When workers are not committed to a job or an organization, it is often because the workers perceive they are not "getting" something equitable from the organization for the work they do. Is the worker getting a fair wage? Is the worker getting health benefits? Does the worker have a good relationship with his or her manager? Is the working environment "comfortable" or at least safe for the employee? Is the worker getting recognition for a job well-done? Is the worker receiving training and development to help him or her succeed in the job?

When these and other worker commitment drivers are deficient or are not provided by organizations, the workers' level of commitment to the job or the organization could fall, leading to reduced effort on the part of the workers and/or reduced odds of job success.

REASON #4: MISALIGNMENT

Misalignment between the organization's goals and those provided in the worker's performance plan

Building on the example of Tab's Donut Shop that I discussed in *Chapter 4: The Anatomy of Job Success*, suppose that I started a business called Tab's Donut Shop and hired two workers, Bob and Ann. To be successful, the donut shop must sell $150,000 in chocolate donuts by the end of the calendar year (the sales goal). To ensure that I sell the requisite amount of chocolate donuts, I cascade (push or allocate) equal parts of that sales goal down to Bob and Ann, so that Bob and Ann are each required to sell $50,000 in chocolate donuts (just as I am). If we each accomplish our individual sales goals of $50,000 in chocolate donuts (for a total of $150,000 in sales), the company will be successful.

By cascading parts of the overall goal down to Bob and Ann and tying their job performance to successfully selling $50,000 in chocolate donuts each, I am driving *alignment* throughout the company – ensuring that we are all focused on accomplishing the same thing: selling chocolate donuts. When I allocate the $50,000 sales goal down to both Bob and Ann, I include that sales goal in their performance plans to ensure that their daily efforts will be focused on achieving the most important thing that they can to help the company succeed: selling $50,000 each in chocolate donuts.

Now suppose that instead of giving Bob a goal of selling $50,000 in chocolate donuts, I, instead, assign him a goal to place 50,000 promotional flyers on the windshields of 50,000 cars by the end of the year to promote the donut shop and, hopefully, drive new business.

It is now the end of the year, and the donut shop is in danger of closing because it was only able to generate

$100,000 in sales of chocolate donuts ($50,000 in sales by Ann and $50,000 in sales by me), NOT the $150,000 in required sales to keep the business running. When I sit down with Ann and Bob for their end-of-year performance reviews, Ann would get a great performance review because she accomplished her defined goal of selling $50,000 in chocolate donuts, and she did *her* part to help the shop succeed. Bob, on the other hand, did not sell any donuts, because he was busy placing flyers onto car windshields. Sure, Bob accomplished his work goal of placing the flyers on windshields. However, his efforts were a waste of time because he did not do his share (sell $50,000 in donuts) to help the donut shop succeed, nor did placing the flyers on car windshields generate $50,000 in sales.

Is it Bob's fault that he was given a goal that had absolutely no impact on helping the donut shop succeed? No. After all, he accomplished his organization-defined goal of placing 50,000 flyers on windshields. The unfortunate reality in many organizations is this: when the organization's leaders gather to debate their worker's performance ratings to determine which workers to get rid of (usually the bottom-rated 5% or something similar), they ask, "Which workers contributed the most to the organization while accomplishing their goals?" During this conversation, managers would conclude that Bob contributed nothing. He would likely be a candidate for involuntary separation, due to no fault of his own. After all, he accomplished the goal that was assigned to him. Unfortunately, the goal that was assigned to him was not aligned with that of the donut shop, meaning his efforts were wasted.

As illustrated in this example, a worker can do a good job of accomplishing the goals and achieving the objectives defined in the worker's performance plan. However, if the goals and objectives are not related to that which is most important to the organization, then the worker's value to the organization could be called into question, positioning the worker to be deemed unsuccessful.

REASON #5: POORLY-CRAFTED GOALS AND OBJECTIVES

Job objectives that are not S.M.A.R.T.

When organizations engage me to help improve their workers' performance, I always start by asking, "How would 'success' be defined and measured for this worker?" At some point, the organization's leadership will get around to showing me the worker's performance plan and explaining how they define success by whether or not the worker successfully achieves the defined objectives stated in the plan; this sounds fine.

The problem arises, however, when I review the objectives. More often than not, the performance plan objectives that I review are ambiguous and do not lend themselves to knowing whether or not a worker has actually achieved these objectives. This never favors the worker, because the worker's success is then based on non-specific factors and could become a popularity contest (deciding on whom success will be bestowed).

So, in addition to ensuring alignment between the business-unit's objectives and the objectives defined for the worker, I also work with the organization to redefine any poorly-developed objectives to ensure they are, indeed, *objective*. This often starts with ensuring that the objectives are specific and measurable, or S.M.A.R.T.

To refresh, objectives should be S.M.A.R.T., or:

- **Specific**: An objective should be clearly-defined and specific enough so that it passes what I refer to as the "fifth-grade test."

- **Measurable**: Measurable objectives, among other things, make it easy to determine whether or not the worker responsible for achieving the objectives did a good job (achieved the objective) or a not-so-good job (did not achieve the objective).

- **Achievable**: When it comes to actually being able to *do* what is required to achieve the objective, the objective should be realistic for that specific worker.

- **Relevant**: The objective, as defined, should be relevant and necessary to contribute to accomplishing the goal with which it is associated.

- **Time-Bound**: Since goals are defined to be accomplished within some specific timeframe (even long-term goals), the objectives that support the goal must also be completed within a given timeframe to ensure that the goal (which is based on completed objectives) can be realized within the established timeframe.

REASON #6: POOR EXECUTION

Execution is the achievement of desired outcomes –usually goals and objectives – through specific, aligned activities. It is about performing tasks that lead to realized initiatives that result in achieved objectives.

Execution is the most important aspect of an organization's or individual worker's strategy, and *workers* are responsible for executing both. An organization's workers, therefore, must have a clear understanding of "Why am I doing this job? What's the point?" They must have a clear understanding of the expectations of them and their individual strategies (performance plans, in the case of the worker).

In many cases, the worker's job objectives are clearly defined, specific, and measurable. Yet, the worker struggles or is unable to achieve the objectives, due in no part to any organizational deficiencies. Typically, the worker does not know how to go about *execution*, or achieving an objective.

There is no hard-and-fast rule to increase one's odds of successfully achieving job objectives. Some people stumble upon success by luck (have you ever heard of a sales "blue bird" – an unexpected "out of the blue" order for goods and services?), whereas others do it through diligence. Whatever one's approach, I prescribe a simple model to increase the chances of workers achieving their objectives:

- Establish clearly-defined, specific, measurable objectives (S.M.A.R.T. objectives). Write them down and keep them in a place where you can review them every day for motivation and focus;

- Determine the *Initiatives* or projects that must be completed to achieve the objectives;

- Identify the tasks that must be finished to complete the Initiatives;

- From the list of possible tasks and to-dos, determine which tasks and to-dos are *priorities*. One way to determine whether a task is important and a priority is to ask, "If I complete this task, will it get me one step closer to completing the associated Initiative and, therefore, one step closer to achieving the associated objective?" If the answer is "yes," then that task should be considered a priority. If the answer is "no," then you will have to decide whether or not completing that task is important in the short-term.

The reason for qualifying the list of possible tasks is

due to the reality that: (a) not all tasks are of equal importance; some are priorities and others are a waste of time; (b) it is unproductive to try to complete every task that is on your task list, because it is inevitable that many of those tasks are unimportant (i.e. by completing them you won't get any closer to achieving your objectives). Completing them is simply a waste of your time; and (c) to be the most productive and achieve your objectives with the least amount of wasted time and effort, qualification ensures that you make the decision to work on *all* priority tasks first and not avoid those that are difficult or dreaded. Decisions lead to action, action leads to progress, progress leads to completions, completions lead to achievement, and achievement ultimately leads to success.

If you get stuck trying to decide which task on the list of *priority* tasks should be completed first, ask yourself this question: "What are the consequences if I do not get this task completed *now*?"

When workers are presented with their annual job objectives at the beginning of the year, many do not know how to create a plan for how they will achieve these objectives. Part of the process of effectively achieving objectives is deciding how the objectives will be achieved, the initiatives/projects and tasks required to complete an objective, and the resources needed (e.g. human capital support, money, and tools, etc.) to complete the tasks within the necessary timeframe.

When organizations do not or cannot provide workers with guidance or assistance to create plans for how the worker can achieve his or her objectives, many (if not most) workers will simply not create a plan, and instead, will resort to performing daily acts of minutiae resulting in nothing of significance.

REASON #7: LACK OF DILIGENCE

While many of the contributors to workers' inability to succeed in their jobs can be attributed to things that are within the direct control of the workers' organization, workers are also culpable for many situations in which they don't succeed. For example, a manager cannot force an uninspired worker to listen, be attentive, follow directions, or complete assignments on time; ultimately, those responsibilities fall into the lap of the worker.

There is an Old English homily that dates back to at least 1775 and states: *Hwa is thet mei thet hors wettrien the him self nule drinken.* Translated it reads: *who can give water to the horse that will not drink of its own accord?* Today, we know this adage as: *You can lead a horse to water, but you can't make him drink it.*

An organization could provide its workers with everything they need to be successful in their jobs – a fair wage, perks and benefits, good leadership, fair and clearly-articulated goals, tools and other resources, development opportunities, support, and a comfortable work environment. Yet, some workers will still find it difficult to succeed in the job because of their own lack of care, hard work, effort, attention to detail, or simply, diligence.

An organization and its leaders can only do so much to promote a worker's job success. Ultimately, it is up to the worker to ensure his or her own success, given the resources available through the organization.

Many things that workers fail to do that contribute to their lack of job success are things that people *should* do naturally when they are hired for any job. You are hired to paint a house? Make sure the paint color is the color the home owner dictated (*listen*); you are hired to design and build a website that includes a shopping cart and a subscription button? Make sure the website includes a working shopping cart and a visible subscription button (*follow instruction*); you are hired to bake three cakes and 12 muffins? Then don't bake only two cakes and 10 muffins and expect to be paid for the job (*complete the assignment*).

One could make the case that the reason why a worker does not follow directions or complete work assignments with the expected degree of quality and completeness is because the worker is potentially disengaged from the job and/or organization. This is something reasonable to consider. My position is this: if a worker spent the resources and effort to find a new job, and the organization ultimately hires the worker for that job and provides all the resources, comforts, and accommodations necessary for the worker to do the job effectively (in other words, the organization does its best to position the worker for success), then a fair exchange would be for you (the worker) to apply the labor necessary to successfully perform the job.

REASON #8: POOR PLANNING

I previously discussed the importance of *execution* (accomplishing goals and achieving objectives) toward job success. Poor execution suggests that a worker either (a) is not clear on what is expected of him or her; (b) does not know how to go about it: deciding which tasks to complete, completing the tasks, or completing initiatives and projects; (c) does not have a plan for how s/he will go about achieving his or her assigned work objectives and accomplishing goals; or (d) all of the above.

In my years of working with individuals on upgrading job performance, I found there is one common thread (among many) that runs through each of these individual situations. They did not have a plan on how they would achieve their objectives and accomplish their goals.

To quote a friend of mine: "One does not plan to be *stupid*, it just happens." Get it?

The meaning behind this quip, one of my all-time favorite quotes, is more complex than it appears on the surface. Superficially, one could read this quote and think it is simply something clever to say to someone who you want to insult. However, when you give it more thought, you will discover that it is really about the significance of planning.

"One does not plan to be *stupid*." This implies that we *do* plan to be the opposite of "stupid" or to avoid reaching some undesirable station, including the one in which we currently find ourselves. Do we want to be at point A (an undesirable one) or do we want to determine how we can reach point B?

" … stupid, it just happens." This implies that if you do not plan for how you will improve your current condition or how you will successfully achieve your job objectives, then you won't. In this context, "stupid" implies some undesirable current state – a place where people with aspirations do not want to be.

Simply put, a *plan* is a roadmap that specifically defines how you will get from A to B; from some current state or condition (that is less than desirable) to some desired state or condition. It is a recipe for how you will succeed. If you are taking a 5-day road trip across the country, you will plan on how to get there safely and efficiently. If you are running for political office, you will create a plan for how you will win the election. If you are baking 10 pies for a big Thanksgiving dinner, you will plan for how you can pull off that feat in your tiny home kitchen. Yet, when you have a job that requires you to achieve 5 objectives, you frequently do not plan on how you will achieve them.

The question is: "why?" The answers can be many, including: "I wasn't told that I have to," or "I'm quite experienced, so I don't need to," or even "Creating a plan is simply a waste of my time." But the most common response is: "I don't know how." Knowing how to develop an effective, executable job-success plan is paramount to achieving sustainable success. To support you in the development of a job-success plan, I have provided a detailed approach for doing so in *Chapter 7: A 10-Step Process Toward Doing Your Job Successfully*.

REASON #9: ORGANIZATION CULTURE

I will admit: I struggle to understand exactly what organization or company "culture" actually means. It's something that everyone acknowledges exists. However, agreeing on exactly what it is remains elusive.

I definitely understand it within the context in which it is most commonly used. But, practically, it doesn't sound too flattering. The reason is because, throughout my travels, workers at all levels within organizations have expressed that they mostly consider "organization culture" to be either a valueless buzzword or a way of acting, thinking, or believing that is inconsistent with their own personal paradigms.

First, there is no such thing as an "organization" per-se, other than in its formal structure. Practically, an organization is simply a collective of *people* that perform various roles and jobs in pursuit of a collective goal. So, when we speak of an organization's "culture," it implies that the culture is the informal, unwritten mores, behaviors, and attitudes held by *workers* within that organization. This makes it seem as if an organization's culture is simply the way people have been compelled to act, as influenced by an organization's leaders. I say that because many organizations take on the character (behaviors – words, expressed attitudes, interactions, and deeds) of their owners or leaders. Within organizations, the words, attitudes, and actions most often mimicked are those that are most visible and influential; those of its leaders. So, in a sense, an organization's culture is simply a reflection of the attitudes and ways of interacting and engaging, as influenced by an organization's leaders. If that is the case, then what does that say about an organization's culture if the organization's leaders are a collective of, say, *bossholes*? You can clearly imagine what the organization "culture" must be like at that organization. And, if you are not cut from the same bosshole-type cloth? Then, this could be considered a "bad organizational fit."

Some say that culture is consistent, observable patterns of behavior in organizations. Some say it's a set of jointly-held beliefs and interpretations about how to do things. And, yet others will say that culture is a force within organizations that promote and reinforce thoughts and behaviors, while sanctioning "wrong" thinking and behaviors (did someone say "groupthink?").

However one defines *culture*, one thing is clear: when a worker thinks or behaves in a manner that differs from the organizational-norm, that worker could be branded as a poor fit, because he or she doesn't align with the organization's "culture." Sometimes, cultural-fit can be a reason why workers are unsuccessful in their jobs, because poor-fit can breed a lack of cooperation, making it harder for a worker to do his or her job effectively.

The term "culture" can be so broadly-defined that it can (and often does) encompass things such as values and personality. This means that almost *any* worker can be characterized as a bad "fit" within an organization.

While organizational culture and fit can be a subject of wide debate, *team fit* is something that is more easily understood.

A *team* is a small group of individuals with complementary skills who must work together to achieve a common purpose for which they hold themselves mutually accountable. Some major responsibilities of team members include:

- Accepts and works toward the goals of the team;
- Attends meetings;
- Participates in meetings;
- Shares their knowledge and expertise;
- Fulfills responsibilities and assigned tasks;
- Practices "beneficial" team behaviors.

If a worker, who is part of a team or is working on a project as a member of a project team, violates any team responsibilities or even fails to "practice beneficial team behaviors," that worker could be considered a poor team-player. Poor team-players run the risk of being ousted from a team and even driven out of an organization if team-violations are considered to be particularly egregious.

I am including "organization culture" as a reason why workers frequently fail in their jobs. The struggle I have with the whole idea of a worker not fitting into an organization's culture is because it is so vague that it gives managers and others the ability to find *any* reason to say that a worker has not done his or her job *successfully* (after all, successful job performance could have subjective elements, such as "values" and "behaviors"), and dismiss the worker for these subjective reasons. Let's face it. In many organizations, "cultural fit" boils down to a popularity contest, and that creates a culture of *likeability,* as opposed to being performance based.

Be that as it may, cultural fit can contribute to a worker's inability to perform his or her job as effectively as possible, often leading to failure.

6

CHAPTER**SIX**

GOOD JOB? BAD JOB? SUCCESSFUL? UNSUCCESSFUL? ARE YOU SURE?

THE PERFORMANCE APPRAISAL / PERFORMANCE MANAGEMENT PROCESS

In their 1996 book, *The Balanced Scorecard: Translating Strategy into Action*, management consultants Robert Kaplan and David Norton defined a scorecard model, the *Balanced Scorecard*, in which they state that, in addition to financial measures, organizational performance should include measures from a customer perspective, an internal business process perspective, and a perspective that measures employee innovation and learning. Performance, they argued, should not simply be based on financial measures, such as revenue, but, instead, should be balanced to include other determinants of how well an organization is truly performing.

The Balanced Scorecard is a planning and management system used by organizations to:

- Communicate what they are trying to accomplish;
- Align the day-to-day work that everyone is doing with strategy;
- Prioritize projects, products, and services; and
- Measure and monitor progress towards strategic targets.

In my experience, organization leaders expect the same from their workers. They want workers to align their day-to-day work with their individual strategic plans (performance plans and associated goals and objectives); prioritize tasks and initiatives/projects to enable them to complete initiatives/projects and achieve their objectives in the most productive and efficient manner; be able to measure and monitor their progress toward achieving their objectives; and communicate their progress with their managers.

And as suggested by the Balanced Scorecard, workers' performance should be measured against multiple criteria that paint a truer picture of how well the worker actually performed as an employee of the organization.

If, as outlined by Kaplan and Norton, an organization measures its performance along financial, customer, internal operations, and learning and development measures – as these goals and objectives are cascaded down throughout the organization – then, ultimately, the workers will have goals and/or objectives that align with the organization's goals and objectives: financial, customer, internal operations, and learning and development. It's logical.

- **Financial measures**: some jobs are more suited to have specific financial objectives in the performance plans of a worker who holds these jobs, such as sales (generate $500,000 in sales this year), finance (reduce Days Sales Outstanding to below 45 days), operations (reduce the spoilage cost by 20%), human resources manager (reduce the attrition cost by 25%), and customer care (reduce the cost of returns by 5% by upselling customers who want to return a product). Other jobs might have indirect financial objectives that, while they don't directly spell out a measurable financial target, achieving them will contribute to an organization's financial performance.

- **Customer measures**: For for-profit and not-for-profit organizations, customers are the lifeblood of the organization; their support is needed for survival and prosperity. Workers in nearly every job function can have many customer-centric goals and objectives. Common options include, such measures as: improve our Net Promoter Score to 9.5 or greater; reduce customer churn by 10%; increase overall customer satisfaction by 12%; or sign up 200 customers for our customer loyalty program.

- **Internal operations measures**: Normally, internal operations measures are about improving processes and efficiency. These objectives could include onboarding new-hires within 30 days, resolving customer service issues within 5 minutes over the phone, and reducing product defects by 15%, for example.

- **Learning and development**: Learning and development goals are designed to ensure that organization leaders maintain a focus on developing its workers to improve engagement, competencies, and performance (among other things). L&D measures might include worker-specific goals, such as obtaining a Six Sigma Green Belt certification or completing the bar exam. Learning and Development department-specific goals might include ensuring alignment between training goals and organizational goals, and achieving a 98%-plus completion rate among workers for the on-line health and safety training course.

My rationale for ensuring that the requirements, goals, and objectives on which workers will be measured are aligned with those of the organization, as a whole, is to show how the four perspectives of the Balanced Scorecard can apply throughout the organization and ultimately to the work-level as well. By doing so, organizations can connect the dots between big picture strategy elements, such as its mission or purpose, strategic focus areas such as its goals, and more operational elements, such as objectives and other Key Performance Indicators (KPIs) which track performance, and initiatives/projects that help workers reach their objectives. This approach removes much of the ambiguity associated with gauging a worker's success, and will give workers the thing that should be a no-brainer: a clear, unequivocal understanding of how they are performing.

This is not easily accomplished given the way most performance management processes and the associated appraisals and reviews are administered, largely due to the highly-subjective nature of the evaluation criteria.

PERFORMANCE MANAGEMENT

A typical performance management review – the official tool by which organizations determine the performance and success of their workers – follows some version of the process outlined below:

- [Ideally] the organization's goals and objectives dictate the most important KPIs that workers are to be measured against (given the worker's specific job functions);

- The organization begins the performance planning process in which a worker's job-specific goals and objectives are defined and other responsibilities and expectations are discussed. The performance management process is also conducted for other purposes, such as providing the basis for making operational and compensation decisions. For this discussion, however, I will focus on those elements that directly impact worker job success;

- [This infrequently happens, but …] Throughout the year, managers provide periodic feedback to the worker as a means of ensuring that the worker is on-track for success. This should be a two-way communication process and, as such, both the worker and manager share responsibility for ensuring that feedback discussions happen;

- The worker provides self-input, which is a form of self-rating on how well the worker believes s/he has performed against the success-criteria defined in the worker's performance plan. This self-input is compared with the manager's ratings and discussed. Then the fun begins;

- The year ends with the official performance review, appraisal, and evaluation, in which the manager makes a final determination on how well the worker performed over a 12-month period and whether or not the worker has performed successfully.

THE PERFORMANCE REVIEW AND APPRAISAL

As a manager, you owe candor to your people.
They must not be guessing about what the
organization thinks of them.

–Jack Welch, former Chairman and CEO
of General Electric

It is not uncommon for workers to wonder – as they walk into their manager's office to discuss their performance and job rating – "Did I do a good job this year? Did I have a bad year? Will my manager think that my job performance this year was successful? I have no way of knowing how this is going to turn out!"

The latter should never be in question. The reason it often *is* in question, however, is because so many of the criteria on which workers are judged are subjective, based on the manager's personal feelings and opinions, and are open to interpretation any way the manager chooses. This is often why a worker might wholeheartedly believe that s/he had done a great job this year, only to receive a performance rating that does not reflect the worker's perception of the year s/he has had.

The performance appraisal commonly contains the following sections or some variant thereof on which workers are evaluated:

Appraisal Criteria	Comments About Objectivity
Achieve goals/objectives/ KPIs	Objective. The rating will be based on data
Skill and proficiency in carrying out assignments	Subjective: Based on opinion and interpretation
Job Knowledge	If a measurable test is administered, objective; otherwise, subjective
Quality of work	If output defects are measured, objective; otherwise, subjective
Quantity of work	If output volumes are measured, objective; otherwise, subjective
Reliability	Subjective: Depends on how it is measured
Initiative and creativity	Good luck trying to measure "creativity"
Communicates effectively	Subjective: Must be specifically-defined
Judgement	Subjective: Based on opinion and interpretation
Cooperation	Subjective: Based on opinion and interpretation
Attendance	Objective. The rating will be based on data
Leadership	Subjective: Based on opinion and interpretation
Planning and organizing	Subjective: Based on opinion and interpretation
Decision-making	Subjective: Based on opinion and interpretation

Admittedly, some of these appraisal criteria can either be objective or subjective based on the characteristics of the criteria and whether there is a specific, measurable element to the criteria. For those criteria for which I believe it is reasonably easy to determine a measurable quality of the criteria, thus making its performance objective, I made a note in the table above.

Taking my evaluation of these common performance appraisal criteria into consideration, it suggests that at least 53% of the criteria on which workers are evaluated are subjective, and another 18% could go either way. This means that **as much as 71% of a worker's performance effectiveness and success could be based on interpretation, personal feelings, and the *opinions* of the worker's manager.**

Such situations are breeding-grounds for debate and disagreements, especially in cases in which organizations provide workers with the ability to provide self-input or self-ratings which are then compared with the manager's ratings. If the manager rates the worker as being less effective than the worker rates him or herself, this can lead to increased defensiveness on the part of the worker, disagreement between the two, and a bad relationship between the two that could negatively impact their abilities to effectively perform. When this occurs, the worker, the manager, and the organization all suffer.

THE POTENTIAL FOR BIAS

While the ideal condition would be for every performance appraisal rating criteria to be cut-and-dry – specific and easily measurable – the reality is that certain aspects of a job are difficult to monitor and, therefore, must be determined by subjective rather than explicit criteria.

The necessity of subjective performance criteria raises issues of systematic bias in organizations' performance management processes, and evidence about the potential for bias in performance appraisals is available from a variety of sources.

In their paper *The Current State of Performance Appraisal Research and Practice: Concerns, Directions, and Implications,* Robert Bretz Jr., George Milkovich, and Walter Read found that, for example, supervisors who had a say in the hiring decision and who viewed the job applicant as favorable subsequently tended to give more favorable performance ratings, whereas those who participated in hiring but viewed the applicant as *unfavorable,* tended to give much less favorable ratings. Also, they found that raters' *expectations* can also introduce bias into the rating process. When behavior was congruent with expectations, appraisal results were more accurate, and disconfirmation of prior expectations appeared to lower ratings. This suggests that managers' expectations introduce error into the performance rating process.

A study by Kurt Kraiger and J. Kevin Ford, which they reported in the paper *A Meta-Analysis of Ratee Race Effects in Performance Ratings*, revealed that the race of the rating-manager and the worker being rated affected evaluations. Overall, managers give higher ratings to subordinates of their own race.

Bias makes it difficult to distinguish genuinely good performance from favoritism.

POTENTIAL CONSEQUENCES OF SUBJECTIVE PERFORMANCE APPRAISAL RATINGS

Many managers perceived no benefit or consequences from conducting thorough performance appraisals, and they see little practical value in doing so.

Multiple surveys have made it clear that managers hate conducting performance reviews. In one survey, 45% of respondents did not see value in the performance review systems they used. Deloitte reported that 58% of HR executives considered reviews an ineffective use of supervisors' time. In addition, in a study by Corporate Executive Board (CEB), the average manager reported spending approximately 210 hours (nearly five weeks) doing performance appraisals each year.

Because of the subjective nature of the evaluation process, the potential for bias, and the fact that the activity is often dreaded by managers (I, too, found the process to be extremely tedious), mistakes and abuses occur, which in turn can become the source of potential legal liability for employers.

For example, an employer's response to reference requests, particularly as they relate to former employees based on performance evaluations, can raise concerns about defamation law suits. Each negative reference provided by an organization based on a worker's poor performance evaluation runs the risk of a defamation suit being initiated by a former worker. For this reason, and the potentially-costly liability, many employers have adopted policies of giving little more than dates of hire and termination in response to job reference requests.

These examples and the study data provide supporting evidence for my contention that the subjective nature of performance appraisals – which are intended to identify development opportunities, gauge worker effectiveness in the job, and dole out compensation – are often simply based on the opinions of rating managers. Because managers' opinions can be biased, workers often find it difficult – if not impossible – to gain an understanding of how well they are truly performing in their jobs and how the organization truly assesses the work they do. And when there is this degree of uncertainty about how a worker is truly performing in his or her job (base on the performance appraisal), the worker cannot effectively determine the steps necessary to improve his or her performance toward being more successful in the job.

7

CHAPTER SVN

A 10-STEP PROCESS
TOWARD DOING YOUR JOB SUCCESSFULLY

ALL IMPROVEMENT REQUIRES CHANGE. If you want to improve your job performance you have to change your approach to how you do your job. This begs the question: how do you know what to change? To gain an understanding of the changes required to perform your job better and more successfully, it is first necessary to understand the levers of your job success. Once the levers are understood, it is then necessary to understand how the levers can impact job performance and success. After gaining this knowledge, it is then necessary to understand what can be done to manipulate the levers in your favor to improve your job performance and perform your job successfully.

Before beginning that quest toward becoming more successful in your job, it is important to understand the anatomy of workers' job-success (the factors that impact job-success and when they are manifested in the employment cycle); detractors from job success; contributors to job success; and the role the performance review and appraisal play in determining job success. This is what I have provided throughout the previous chapters of this book.

Without understanding and appreciating the factors and conditions that have a bearing on whether or not a worker is successful in his or her job, any effort to improve job performance would be inefficient and likely unsuccessful. It is difficult, if not impossible, to improve the performance of an automobile if you don't know all of the factors that impact an automobile's performance and which factors to manipulate to upgrade automotive performance.

The *10-Step Process Toward Doing Your Job Successfully* that I outline below is based on a comprehensive understanding of the factors that impact job performance and success, how to manipulate those factors to produce the desired outcome – job-success – and proven, practical methodologies and practices that provide workers with the best chance of achieving job-success.

A 10-STEP PROCESS
TOWARD DOING YOUR JOB SUCCESSFULLY

STEP 1: UNDERSTAND WHAT YOUR JOB *REALLY* IS

The job of the chef is not *to cook*. If it were that simple, then my 14-year-old son would be a chef, because – without regard for taste, quality, or degree-of-doneness – he "cooks." No. The chef's job is to ensure the gastronomic satisfaction of diners.

The job of the math teacher is not to teach students math. If it were that simple, then *I* am a math teacher, because I teach my 11-year-old son math. No. According to the National Council of Teachers of Mathematics, the role of the math teacher is to inspire students to look beyond the pages of their textbook to become problem-solvers and critical thinkers.

When the chef understands that his or her role is not to simply *cook*, but is, instead, to ensure diners' satisfaction, s/he has a better appreciation for the things that s/he must do to achieve these outcomes. When the chef realizes this, s/he will then begin to think about all the things that are required to ensure that diners have a memorable dining experience, so much so that diners will seek out that chef even if the chef moves restaurants to receive that culinary experience.

"Chef" means "Chief" in French; the head of the kitchen. It has nothing to do with food (unless, for example, the type of chef is specified, like chef de cuisine, or the "chief of food"). Americans, however, are accustomed to equating the title "chef" with "cook."

The chef is responsible for many things, including:

- Preparing menus and new dishes, and ensuring that pricing is appropriate for diners and the restaurant;
- Guaranteeing that staff are trained, especially in food portion sizes and presentation;
- Working with purchasing companies on food orders;
- Ensuring that all food and necessary materials are in stock and stored in the proper conditions; and
- Maintaining excellent cooking skills.

While this list of responsibilities is not exhaustive, it provides you with a better appreciation of how the chef will organize and manage his or her day, and the kinds of things s/he will have to be capable of if s/he is to do the job successfully; it is significantly different than if the chef thought that his or her job was simply *to cook*.

If the chef thought his or her job was simply to cook, that chef would think that all s/he needed to do was cook good food, and that this would make him/her successful. The reality is: that chef would fail badly in his or her job.

The enlightened chef, however – one who understands

that the chef's job is multi-faceted – will understand that to do the job successfully, s/he will have to ensure that the menus, new dishes, kitchen staff, food quality, food prices and profit margins, and, yes, the food, are all excellent. The chef understands that to deliver exceptional food-focused dining experiences all these things must come together.

Understanding what your job *really* is – its purpose – should be the first order of business for workers, especially those newly-hired into their organizations. Once you understand why you were hired, you can then start to map your skills and experiences with those required for the job; this will help you identify potential job-fit gaps. This mapping should force you to ask yourself, "How can I execute my job responsibilities so that I can successfully fulfill the purpose of the job? Is it possible for me to fulfill that purpose based on the stated job responsibilities?"

One thing that I recommend for gaining great insight into how to begin the pursuit of your job success is to speak with a person or people who have previously held the job (if they are available) and have performed it successfully. Pick their brains about best-practices and pitfalls. There is also value in asking your boss and others in-the-know about the person or people who have held the job and were *unsuccessful*. Find out why they failed and add that to your mental Rolodex of things *not* to do.

Recommendations:

- Understand the true purpose of your job. What were you really hired to do?

- Complete this sentence: If I do my job successfully, the value that I will provide to this organization is

  _____.

- Map your skills and experience against the job responsibilities to identify gaps.

- Understand whether or not you would be successful in the job if you *only* executed (successfully) the job requirements, as stated. If you determine that you cannot be successful by doing so, then use the value of the experiences of your predecessors and your boss to understand what *really* is needed to do the job successfully.

- Speak with your job's predecessors who have performed the job successfully, and learn from the mistakes of those who have performed the job unsuccessfully. Add this insight into your job-success plan.

STEP 2: UNDERTAKE AN HONEST INVENTORY OF YOUR CURRENT STATE AND PERFORM A GAP ANALYSIS

One of the most uncomfortable, and as a result, difficult, things for workers to do is to acknowledge that they don't know something. In the workplace, this could be an acknowledgement that they don't know how to successfully perform their jobs. Sure, we could look at the job description that has been developed for our role and note the job duties and responsibilities of the job we hold. Then, we could compare our skills, experience, and capabilities against those requirements, identify the duties and responsibilities we believe we can fulfill, and make an assumption about how well we would do. Or we could reach into the reservoir of our self-confidence and say that, even if we don't yet know how to successfully do our job, we are capable enough to figure it out. However, without a plan for how to get from our current job-state to a successful job-state (assuming we are not currently at that state), the odds of our succeeding go down dramatically.

Before workers can begin to chart a course to get from where they are today to where they want to be, they must first articulate the end-state: where they want to *be*. The goal-state. Job success. Next, they must identify the "barriers" that stand between these two states; what separates the worker from achieving job success? The barriers, or *roadblocks* – those things that, if they were eliminated, would enable you to successfully perform your job – can appear as two general types: TAS- (talent, ability, skill) gap barriers and job-success plan barriers.

Job-success plan barriers refer to the worker's inability to execute elements of a job-success plan. TAS-gap barriers—reviewed in greater detail below—are deficiencies in our level of talent, our abilities, and/or our skill levels that inhibit us from achieving job-success.

This begs the question: what is the difference between talent, ability, skill, and experience? Simply:

- A skill is something that is learned which can later be applied productively.

- Talent, on the other hand, is something that is naturally developed in a person, through heredity and external stimuli.

- Ability is the capacity of a person to do a certain thing. It is a by-product of experience, skills, and/or talent. Ability is synonymous with capability.

- Experience is the state of having been affected by or gained knowledge through direct, personal observation, or participation; it is akin to learning, and it feeds skills, ability, and talent.

Talent-, Ability-, Skill- (TAS) Gap Barriers

After listing and reviewing your job duties and responsibilities, you should then undertake an honest inventory of your talents, ability, and skills to determine which of the requisite duties and responsibilities you believe you are capable of satisfying and which you do not believe you can satisfy. The duties and responsibilities that you cannot satisfy or perform become *barriers* to your job success. And the deficiencies or *holes* in your skill set and ability are identified as TAS-gap barriers.

For example, if one of your primary job responsibilities is to translate documents written in Mandarin into English, but you do not speak the most common Chinese language, you will have a language skill-gap barrier that prevents you from doing your job successfully.

Identifying the TAS-gaps becomes a question of, "Based on the duties and responsibilities of this position, what skills and capabilities do/will I *need* to be successful in this job?" and "what skills and capabilities do I *have?*" Before a gap can be closed, these two questions must be answered. The gaps must be identified, and a plan must be put in place to close the gaps.

Gaps are barriers or roadblocks to success. If you want to get from your current job performance state to your desired job performance, you must eliminate these barriers (close the gaps).

GAPS = Barriers and Roadblocks to Success

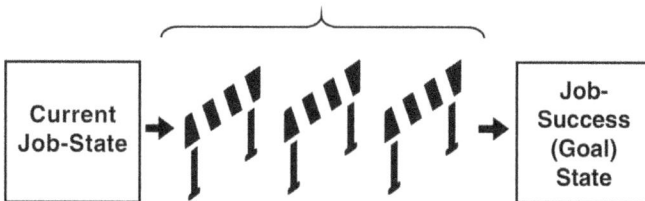

So, if you want to close your Mandarin-speaking TAS-gap so that you can translate the documents effectively and become successful in your job, you must acquire the skill of – at least – reading Mandarin.

A **Gap Analysis** is the process of acknowledging that TAS-gaps exist, identifying the gaps and their causes, establishing the impact of a closed-gap on job performance (if there *will* be a change), and determining what will be required for you to close the gaps. One of my recommended approaches for performing a gap analysis and developing a plan to close any identified, impactful gaps is *difference-reduction.*

The idea behind difference-reduction as a gap-closing/barrier-eliminating approach is that there can be significant differences between a worker's current job-state and his or her desired goal-state. The only way the worker can achieve his or her desired job-goal-state is to reduce and eliminate the number of *differences* (roadblocks) that exist between the two states.

Using the Mandarin document translation job requirement as an example, the worker has performed a gap analysis. S/he has acknowledged that s/he cannot perform this aspect of his or her job; s/he has identified the reason why (s/he cannot speak or read Mandarin); s/he has determined that the ability to read and translate Mandarin documents into English is critical to his or her job success (a *critical success factor*), and s/he has identified a solution to close the TAS-gap (learning to read Mandarin). The employee has put a plan in place to do this, thus eliminating this barrier to his or her job success.

In this example, the difference between the worker's current job-state (not being able to translate important documents) and his or her job-state goal (to be able to successfully translate the Mandarin documents into English) is the ability to speak and/or read Mandarin. By learning to read and speak Mandarin – and reducing (eliminating) this difference between the two states – the worker will be able to successfully perform this aspect of his or her job.

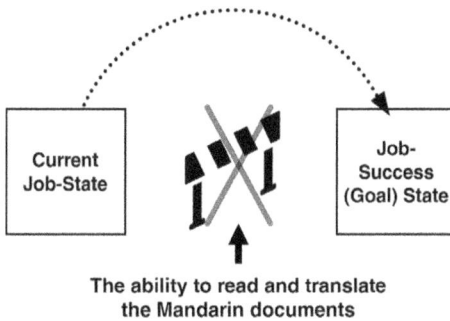

The ability to read and translate
the Mandarin documents

A job success plan begins with an understanding of the goal(s) you are charged with achieving and knowing what gets in the way of you accomplishing the goal(s). By performing a gap analysis, you will be able to:

- Define and document your job duties and responsibilities;
- Identify those duties and requirements that you cannot satisfy (TAS-gaps);
- Determine the gravity and impact (on your job performance) of not being able to perform the above-mentioned activities;

- Narrow down what will enable you to successfully perform these gap-duties and responsibilities; and

- Develop a plan to gain the skills necessary to perform the gap-duties and responsibilities.

Recommendations:

- Perform a gap analysis.

- Document the comprehensive list of job duties and responsibilities that you are charged with performing this year.

- Undertake an honest inventory of your talents, ability, and skills as they relate to your ability to successfully perform your job responsibilities.

- Identify and document the gaps that exist between your job-duties and your capability to perform them; in other words, highlight the duties and responsibilities that you cannot perform.

- Determine what is needed for you to close the TAS-gaps and successfully perform the duties.

- Document that which is needed and, working with your manager, develop an actionable learning and development plan that will enable you to acquire the necessary skills and knowledge for you to successfully perform the job duties and responsibilities.

STEP 3: ENSURE THAT THE OBJECTIVES YOU ARE CHARGED WITH ACHIEVING (TO HAVE A SUCCESSFUL YEAR) ARE *S.M.A.R.T.*

An objective is the clear articulation of the thing(s) that must be achieved to succeed. Job-related work objectives are the clear articulation of the thing(s) a worker must achieve for the worker to be considered to have had a successful year. They are the performance criteria that workers are evaluated against. Therefore, an organization's specific expectations must be clearly defined in the objectives for a worker to be able to implement them.

Objectives should also be agreed upon by both the worker and manager. Goal- and objective-setting should be participatory; both the worker and manager are involved in their development to ensure an absolute understanding of and commitment to them.

Done properly, work objectives motivate employees to a higher level of performance and focus the worker's efforts on that which is most important in their jobs. Setting clearly-defined, specific, and measurable work objectives is critical to the worker achieving the desired performance results. When you consider that a worker's success at achieving his or her objectives (their *performance* as determined by the ratings that the worker receives in her or his performance review and appraisal process) is used to support decisions related to career development, compensation, promotions, and reductions-in-force or employment termination, it becomes even more critical that work objectives are super clear, specific, measurable, realistically-achievable by the worker, understood, and agreed upon.

Done poorly, however, the worker would not know the criteria on which their job performance is being measured. Not only can this be de-motivating, but it can also contribute to a worker's poor job performance due to the potential that the worker may be extremely unproductive.

Productivity is the degree to which one is able to achieve a desired outcome or *produce* some pre-defined result while considering the impact on resources. Doing productive work – work that contributes to a worker's progress toward accomplishing goals and achieving objectives – contributes to job success; it is about getting important things done. "Important," in this context, relates to those activities that, if the worker completes them, will get the worker one step closer to achieving his or her objectives. This suggests that, by the worker focusing his or her efforts on completing the most important activities in his or her workday, the worker will waste less time completing value-less busy-work, and will achieve her or his objectives more quickly and effectively by focusing their efforts directly on achieving objectives.

S.M.A.R.T. objectives drive focus and productivity. Ambiguous objectives drive wasted effort. If objectives are *specific*, they will not cause confusion; if objectives are *measurable*, you will know whether or not you have achieved them; if it is realistically-*achievable* by you, you will buy into it, because it is do-able; if it is *relevant* to an associated goal, you know there is alignment and it is worthwhile; and if it is *time-bound*, you will know when you need to achieve the outcome.

I recall a work objective that was assigned to a client with whom I was working to help him become more successful in his job. As always, I started by looking at his work objectives. Imagine my surprise when I read one that stated: "Become well-known and highly-respected within the industry." Let's analyze this "objective." And, for the analysis, let's break this objective into two parts and analyze each one separately.

Part 1: "Become well known within the industry." What does it mean to be "well-known?" How many people will have to know you for you to be considered "well" known? Which people or types of people will have to know you for you to be considered well "known"? What if you believe that you are already "well-known?" Does that mean you don't need to do any work this year related to this objective? And, even taking into account the Cambridge English Dictionary definition of well-known ("known or recognized by many people"), there is still no clarity.

Part 2: "Become highly-respected within the industry." As with Part 1, what does it mean to be "respected," let alone "highly"-respected? Since the respect that someone has for another person is an individual and subjective *feeling*, are you comfortable basing your salary, job, and livelihood on someone else's *feelings*?

It should be obvious that with poorly-defined "objectives," such as these, it is impossible to ascertain whether or not they have been successfully achieved. Unless this objective has been clearly defined with a measurable element, there will be disagreement, debate, and the potential for bad blood between the worker and manager, as happened in this situation.

Ensuring Clarity

Whenever I review workers' work objectives as part of the improvement process, I start by asking the workers two simple questions about each objective:

1. How will you know, unequivocally, that this objective has been successfully achieved?

2. During the performance review and appraisal meeting between you and your manager, will you both completely agree about your success at achieving this objective and to the degree to which you have achieved it?

Your answers to these two questions will be the first step in determining whether or not your work objectives are well-defined, as well as in your and the organization's best interests.

For a worker to successfully perform his or her job, the worker and manager must know and agree on whether or not an objective has been successfully achieved by the worker. If it has not been, then **the onus is on the worker to ensure that the objective is re-crafted,** such that it is S.M.A.R.T. and the answers to the two questions above are "easily" and "yes," respectively.

But, how do you go about re-crafting an objective to ensure that it is well-defined? It's simple. For each objective, ask two questions: *How much* and *by when?*

If, for example, a worker's initially-drafted objective is "to improve sales within the region," asking "how much and by when" will force a discussion between the worker and manager about how to *measure* the desired sales improvement outcome and when that outcome is expected to be achieved. So, the objective could then be re-drafted as "to improve sales *by $100,000 over last year's sales* within the region." While this represents a good start, it still leaves a question about what boundaries will represent the "region."

At this point, I recommend following up with an additional question: *Is every parameter clearly defined and specific? If not, clarify and specify them.*

By asking this question, it forces the worker and manager to look at each aspect of the objective and to ensure its clarity. In this example, "... within the *region*" requires clarification and specificity. It might be re-crafted more specifically as "… within the East region that encompasses the Mid-Atlantic States of New York, New Jersey, Pennsylvania, Delaware, and Maryland."

Then, as needed, I will follow up with another question: *Is the objective S.M.A.R.T.?*

Comparing the two objectives – the originally-stated objective and the re-crafted objective – we find that one is *subjective* and ambiguous, and the other is, as the name implies, *objective*:

- **Original**: "To improve sales within the region"

- **Re-crafted**: "To improve sales by $100,000 over last year's sales, within the East region, encompassing the Mid-Atlantic States of New York, New Jersey, Pennsylvania, Delaware, and Maryland by 12/31/20XX."

Question: Which of these two versions of the work objective would you feel most clear and comfortable pursuing, knowing that your performance will be based on it?

The necessity of goal- and objective-clarity is even more important (and challenging) for workers in managerial positions, since the stakes are higher and the potential impact of failure is greater (because, for one thing, it would possibly impact more people). What if, for example, a worker's job is managerial? Managers develop and manage people (and are held responsible for their subordinates' performance), build coalitions, allocate resources, and decide upon go-forward actions. The manager is also a figurehead, representative, networker, and information disseminator. How do you measure *these* activities and performance criteria in a performance plan?

Remember: *facts trump opinion.* In addition, if you cannot measure something, you cannot improve it. Your job performance should be based on objective facts, not your supervisor's *opinion* about how well you performed. Also, the performance management process is partly about improving workers' performance and capabilities. To upgrade a worker's performance, it is necessary to be able to *measure* their desired performance; this requires specific and measurable criteria within their work objectives.

My experience working with individuals and organizations of all types in countries around the world has shown me that, when it comes to creating a worker's goals and objectives for his or her performance plan, many managers did not place much focus on ensuring that goals and objectives are S.M.A.R.T. Therefore *you*, the worker, must act in your own self-interest and ensure that each and every work objective is well-defined, since your success hinges on them. I recommend that, until they *are* well-defined, workers do not sign off on the performance plan. This action should force a discussion with the necessary parties about clarifying subjective "objectives."

Recommendations:

- Do not sign off on or approve a performance plan if the work objectives that you are charged with achieving are not S.M.A.R.T. Recommend that your boss (and even Human Resources, as appropriate) agree to work with and collaborate with you on crafting objectives that you understand, are aligned with, and agree to.

- For each objective ask three specific questions: (1) "How much and by when," to help quantify goals and define a time parameter; (2) "Is every parameter clearly defined and specific?" If not, clarify and specify; and (3) "Is the objective S.M.A.R.T.?" These questions should also be asked about the other performance criteria, including "Behavioral" Goals, Performance Competencies, Duties, and Success Criteria and other desired outcomes contained within a typical performance plan.

- To upgrade productivity and achieve higher success rates and more quickly, identify important, priority activities on which you should spend your time. To do this, each day compile a list of your tasks and to-dos. Then, from that list, determine those activities that are priorities by asking about each activity: "If I complete this activity, will it get me one step closer to achieving my goal or objective?" If the answer is yes, then the activity is important; if the answer is no, then you will have to determine whether or not it is worthwhile to complete.

Another question you can ask to help you determine which activities are the most important, requiring that they be completed quickly, is: "What would be the consequences if I did not do this activity now or today?" Those activities with the most significant consequences – either good or bad – are priorities; complete them first. By prioritizing your activities, tasks, and to-dos to focus on completing the most important items, you will then have the ability to track your progress toward achieving your objectives. For each important activity you complete, you should get a step closer to achieving your objectives. Because these objectives are now measurable, you can track your progress by the number of activities you have completed.

After you have determined which activity(ies) on your list are important and/or priorities, place them on your calendar to ensure that you allocate time to complete them. There is a significantly-greater likelihood that you will actually do something if you put that activity on your calendar.

STEP 4: DOCUMENT YOUR GOALS AND OBJECTIVES AND MAKE THEM VISIBLE; REVIEW THEM DAILY

Every day, workers are greeted with a list of activities, tasks, and to-dos that could consume the entirety of a workday. And even then, there is no guarantee that the worker will complete all the activities on his or her to-do list. Besides, workers should not *want* to complete every activity on their to-do list, because it is inevitable that many of these activities are value-less and a complete waste of time.

The most successful people are driven by accomplishing goals. The goal-related characteristics of people who are the most effective at accomplishing these goals include:

- They clearly define and document the goals to which they aspire;

- They place these goals someplace where they can view them each and every day. By maintaining daily visibility of their goals, successful people then look at the list of activities they could spend their time working on in any given day. They can then ask themselves the previously stated qualifying question for each activity on their to-do list: If I spend time completing this activity, will its completion get me a step closer to accomplishing my goal? If the answer is yes, then they allocate their time to getting these priority activities done.

Maintaining daily-visibility of one's goals and objectives *drives the discipline* of ensuring that – of all the things you *could* spend your time on during the course of a day – you spend your time completing activities that have the greatest impact on your success; success is defined as the accomplishment of your goals and/or the achievement of your objectives.

Recommendations:

- Ensure that your goals are clearly articulated and your objectives are clearly defined and S.M.A.R.T.;

- Document your goals/objectives so that they can be captured, stored, and easily retrieved, as needed;

- Place a copy of the goals/objectives in a place where you can maintain visibility of them at least once per day. Some people place these goals on their bathroom mirror; some people place them on their computer and/or phone as their start-up screens, and others place them on the front cover of their notebooks; and

- Use your goals and objectives to qualify your daily list of activities, tasks, and to-dos and determine which of them are important; priorities. Do this by asking about each activity: If I complete this activity, will it get me closer to accomplishing my goal or achieving my objective?

STEP 5: DEVELOP A PLAN
FOR HOW YOU WILL ACHIEVE A "MAKE"

If you are going away on a two-day trip to a specific
destination on a specific date, you don't just jump
into your car and start driving aimlessly.

—Tab Edwards, on the importance of planning

Many years ago, when I was a rookie salesman taking over my first sales territory, I attended my first individual sales planning session. The sessions were held at the beginning of the year for each sales person, and the outcome of the planning session was to "show a 'make.'"

At the time, I wondered, just as I imagine you are wondering, what is a "make?" As my then-manager explained to me: "Now that you are a *real* salesman and no longer a trainee, you have been assigned a sales quota (objective) that you are expected to deliver by the end of the year. Imagine this: you are standing on the edge of a riverbank and a major storm is approaching. You must figure out a way to successfully get to the other side of the 4-mile wide river within 3 days to reach safety from the approaching storm. How will you get to the other side of the river in 3 days? In other words, what is your *plan* that shows how you will 'make it' from where you stand today to where you must get to? Be specific."

As it turned out, showing a "make" was simply another way of saying that I had to come up with a plan that specifically defined (showed) what I could do to achieve (make) my annual sales quota. In addition to defining each specific activity that would lead to achieving my sales goal, I also had to identify the resources (assistance from other workers, marketing budget, technology, time, etc.) that would be necessary for me to successfully complete the identified activities.

Over the years, I have found that managers at all types of organizations use the term "showing a make" when instructing their (most often) sales professionals to create a plan to achieve sales success.

The end result of the aforementioned planning session would be the creation of a detailed plan that showed my organization's upper-managers exactly how I planned to *make* my sales quota, or achieve success.

An Action Plan

A "plan" is a "strategy" and a strategy is a plan. Whichever term is used, they are both roadmaps for getting you from point-A (the edge of a riverbank) to point-B (safety on the other side of the river). By definition, a strategy is a *plan* to achieve objectives – measurable targets that have been established to help you accomplish your goals and aspirations, and determine whether or not you are successfully achieving them.

Objectively defining your goals, objectives, and/or aspirations should be the starting point for your job-success initiative; every meaningful activity in which you engage should be dictated by the goal(s) that you are trying to accomplish or objective(s) you are trying to achieve. To put it in terms of a roadmap, the goal is the destination and the associated objectives provide a quantifiable measure of how you will know that you have arrived at the goal. Once you know where you are trying to go, you can then map out the best route to get there.

This is the reason why every organization's performance plan includes goals and/or objectives that indicate what is expected of their workers if the workers are to be considered to have performed their jobs successfully.

After you have established a job goal and the associated objectives that quantitatively and specifically determine if the goal has been accomplished, the next step is to do something to achieve the objectives and, consequently, the associated goal. This introduces the concept of an **"Action Plan."**

An *action plan* is a plan of action for how you will achieve a goal or objective. It answers the question: What specific initiatives, activities, action items, and/or tasks must be completed to realize the goal or objective?

Action Planning

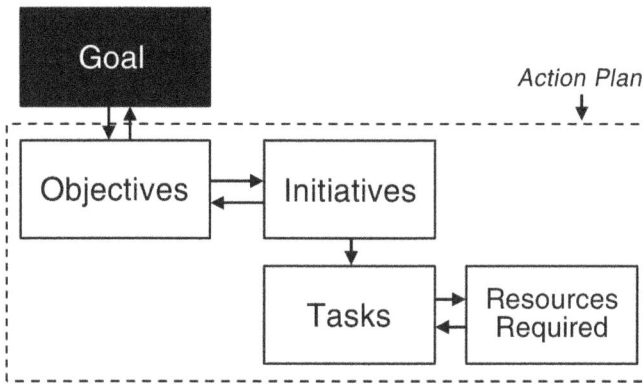

The #1 reason why plans and strategies fail is because of poor plan execution. It is not enough to simply *want* to do your job successfully, you must also perform the job activities necessary to achieve that success. In other words, you must *execute* your plan or strategy.

Execution means accomplishing the action items and tasks that you have determined are necessary to complete the defined initiatives and, ultimately, achieve your objectives.

The Cause-and-Effect Nature of a Plan

Effective plans or strategies contain relationships that follow cause-and-effect logic, ruling out coincidence (as much as possible). Cause-and-effect supposes that if you do "A" then "B" will happen as a direct result of having done "A." This is illustrated in the diagram below. If you do not do "A," however, then "B" will not happen.

This "if-then" nature of strategy holds that once we undertake an action, we expect that the outcome of the action (an outcome we predicted would occur before we took the action) actually occurs. In a well-developed plan, this cause-and-effect relationship will exist between goals and objectives; objectives and initiatives; and initiatives and tasks.

**The Cause-and-Effect Relationships
Between the Elements of a Plan**

An example of causation (cause-and-effect) is turning on a light switch: when you flip a light switch, the light comes on. And if you flipped the light switch 100 times, the light would come on 100 times. The light coming on (the effect) is a direct result of you turning on the light switch (the cause of the light coming on). It is also safe to assume that if you did not turn on the light switch, then the light would not go on.

Analogously, it's like tipping dominoes: if you line up ten dominoes in a row, with the *goal* of knocking down the tenth domino, and you tip the first domino into the second one, that initial tip (the cause) would ultimately result in the second, third, fourth, fifth … and ultimately, the tenth domino falling down (the effect; the desired outcome).

Coincidence, on the other hand, supposes that if you do "C" then "D" happens. However, "D" could have happened even if you did not do "C." Therefore, the "D" event is a coincidence, because it randomly happened immediately after you did "C," and its occurrence was not related to the "C" event. For example, every time I wear my lucky socks to the game, my team wins! No, wearing my "lucky" socks did not *cause* my team to win the game; it is just coincidence.

The "if-then" nature of planning holds that once we take an action, we expect that the outcome of the action actually occurs. If it does, then we consider the next action that we engage in will get us another step closer to achieving an objective and/or accomplishing a goal. Plans that are developed without cause-and-effect relationships are poorly developed, and their execution would not necessarily equal progress toward achieving the plan's goals and objectives. It must be noted that, even if a worker gets the strategy "right" and even if he or she carries it out efficiently and effectively, all the worker can hope for is that the odds are in his or her favor that the strategy will be effectively executed, resulting in its desired outcomes.

So, as you develop a plan to show how you will achieve job success, you should do your best to ensure that the activities you define as being necessary to achieve your work objectives will directly result in (cause) the objectives to be achieved. This will help you identify **priority** (the most important) activities, tasks, and to-dos on which you should spend your time.

Adjustments

The quantitative and/or measurable nature of objectives enables you to determine whether or not you are making progress toward achieving your objectives. This is a good thing because, as you measure your progress, if you find that you are not making improvements or getting closer to achieving your objectives, you can modify necessary elements of your plan to get back on-track. For this reason, a plan should be a "living" document. As such, it should be continually monitored, edited, and updated, based on the conditions surrounding you and the factors that impact your pursuit of the plan.

Plans are naturally modified over time. So, when you find that it is necessary to make adjustments to the plan, do not panic; every successful plan that I have ever developed for a company, organization, or individual – and I have done hundreds – was modified at some point (or even at multiple points). Adjustments to a plan should not always be seen as something negative. If, for example, after measuring your progress toward achieving a plan objective you find that you are way ahead of schedule, then adjusting the plan to reflect the fact that you are doing so well is great; it means that you will begin reaping the rewards of an accomplished goal sooner than originally hoped.

Initiatives

As you develop your job-success plan, you might wonder, "What is that stage that may exist between a work objective and a set of activities, tasks, and to-dos that I created to achieve the objective?" I refer to that link as an *initiative*. An initiative is a project or program undertaken to achieve specific objectives in the near-term. Based on this definition, some people use the terms *initiatives* and *projects* interchangeably.

Initiatives are influenced by objectives, and they *identify* and *define* the undertakings that must be fulfilled for objectives to be realized in the short- (within 12 months) or near-term (often within 18 months). Initiatives are often considered to be *critical success factors*.

Critical success factors (CSFs) are the few key areas of activity that must absolutely be successfully completed for a worker to achieve her or his objectives. CSFs represent the *factors* that are *critical* to the *success* of the worker charged with achieving certain objectives. Within the plan's framework, the elements that are critical success factors for the worker to accomplish his or her work objectives are most often **initiatives**.

There is a nuanced difference between an initiative and a task. An easy way to understand this difference is by asking the qualification question: "Is this an activity that I can complete as one, single activity, or will completion of this activity require multiple steps or tasks." Consider the activity of *cleaning out the garage*. While *cleaning out the garage* can be considered to be an activity, when we consider it further by asking the qualification question, we find that, to have a clean garage, there are multiple steps or *tasks* that are required. These steps or tasks could include throwing out the trash, giving away old bikes and toys, cleaning the oil off the ground, and sweeping the floor. After having completed all these tasks, the result would be a clean garage. In this example, the garage would be considered a multi-step initiative or project, and *not* a single-activity task.

As it relates to job-specific work objectives, for example, if a worker has been charged with the goal or objective to "reduce voluntary employee attrition by 10% compared with the prior year's rate," the worker might define several initiatives to achieve that goal/objective, and the tasks required to complete the initiatives as follows:

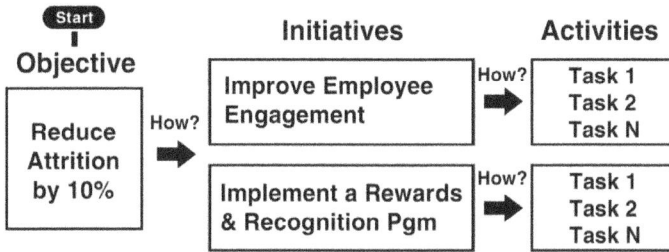

To make it easy for you to develop a job-success plan, I have provided a full-size *Job-Success Plan Workbook* on the website www.TabEdwards.com, and I have included a copy of the plan workbook in the Appendix of this book.

Recommandations:

- Develop a plan to "show a make:" Create a job-success plan that outlines how you will achieve your job-related work objectives; having work objectives is pointless if you are not serious about achieving them. If you are, however, serious about achieving them then you must determine how you can do it. The plan should include your work objectives, the initiatives / projects that must be completed to achieve the objectives, and the tasks that must be wrapped up to complete the initiatives.

- Use the *Job-Success Plan Workbook*: To facilitate your job-success planning efforts, I have provided a workbook that takes you step-by-step through the plan-creation process. The workbook and all necessary forms are provided in the Appendix, and a downloadable, full-size version of the workbook is available at the website www.TabEdwards.com.

- Identify Critical Success Factors / Initiatives: Initiatives identify and define the undertakings that must often be fulfilled for objectives to be realized. Initiatives are often considered to be *critical success factors*. Critical success factors (CSFs) are activities that absolutely must be completed for a worker to achieve her or his objectives. CSFs/initiatives can be identified by asking this three-part question:

  (1) What are the major activities or *things* that must be completed for me to reach this objective?

  (2) If I complete all these activities or *things*, will I reach the objective? If the answer is "no," then you must add different or additional potential initiatives until the answer – based on your learned belief, which may include the supporting opinion of others – is "yes."

  (3) If I *do not* complete a specific activity or thing, will I get any closer to reaching my objective? If the

answer is "no," then it is likely a well-defined initiative. If the answer is "yes," then that activity is probably not necessary for you to spend time completing.

- Apply "If-Then" logic: Ensure that cause-and-effect logic is built into your "make" plan, such that completing your important action items, tasks, and to-dos will result in completed initiatives or projects, and completed initiatives/projects will result in achieving your objectives.

- Adjust: Review the plan daily (or weekly at the very least) and adjust the plan as necessary based on new learnings, obstacles, delays, or other factors that impact the successful completion of your initiatives and/or the achievement of your objectives.

STEP 6: WORK PRODUCTIVELY

Productivity relates to getting important things done. And those *important things* that workers strive to get done are their job-related work objectives. To be productive is to *produce* or achieve some pre-defined outcome – typically goals and objectives.

While there are different types of productivity – technological productivity which refers to the more efficient use of tools, machinery, and technology to increase output; and managerial productivity which focuses on the manager's ability to run a business better than before – I will focus on *worker productivity*: their ability to achieve the objectives and accomplish the goals that have been defined for their specific jobs.

Most organizational leaders will acknowledge that there are many different types of work, such as "busy work," in which the worker simply does any and everything that s/he can fit into a workday, regardless of whether or not the activities are a waste of time. There is also "brownie work," (based on the 1950s term "brown-nosing") in which the worker primarily focuses on doing those things that, whether they are wasteful or not, will curry favor with a person or people the worker is trying to suck up to or impress. Then, there is the "hard work," which we have all been instructed to do from the time we were kids.

There are several problem with "hard work," including that no one knows exactly what it really means to work "hard." I guess you can say that it simply means to put forth your best effort to perform a task or do a job. However, working hard does not equate with working smarter or more productively. It simply means that you are putting forth maximum effort, even if the effort is directed at things that are a waste of time.

To be clear, hard work is not confined to physical labor. Every day in professional offices, schools, coffee shops, and pubs, workers and others in those environments say that they are "working hard." My experience has been that, when people in certain lines of work make this claim, what they mean is that they are *busy*. When a teacher says that he is "working hard," he might mean that he is *busy* grading lots of exams before the submission deadline. When a barista says that she is "working hard," it might be that she is *busy* pulling 20 double espressos for impatient customers. But when workers in other lines of work say they are "working hard," they might mean that they are performing certain acts that are physically demanding, such as baking coal in 3,000-degree ovens to make coke.

For this discussion, I am not necessarily focusing on hard work, or busy work, or brownie work. I am focusing on *productive* work: getting the most important things done in the shortest amount of time, with the highest degree of quality (e.g. few mistakes), while consuming the fewest resources.

Detractors from Productivity (and Considerations for addressing the Detractors)

1. Managers

Often, a manager will delegate assignments to workers that are – by definition – unrelated to the workers' success and not priorities for them. As a result, workers will spend lots of time performing activities that do not help them achieve their work objectives, thereby wasting their valuable time.

Consideration:

If the manager's request is not related to helping you successfully perform your job, you should consider delegating the request to someone else, asking the requestor whether someone else on the team can complete the activity, or discussing with your manager that, by completing the unrelated activity, you will be taken away from activities that the organization has identified as being the most important things for you to do.

While it can be very hard for a worker to push-back against a manager's request, it is professionally fair to ask this of a manager or anyone else who may request that you perform activities that do not align with the most important things that you must get done (for you to be successful).

2. Technology

The promise of technology was that it would improve user productivity. While technology has delivered on this promise to a degree, it has also detracted from productivity, specifically when you consider the time wasted using collaboration tools and social applications.

Entrepreneur Magazine published the results of a recent survey of U.S. workers in sales, marketing, human resources, and legal departments. This survey found that email, text and instant-messaging, switching between applications, and checking personal social networking sites account for nearly 60% of work interruptions. The survey also found that 45 percent of surveyed workers said they could not work 15 consecutive minutes without an interruption. Another 53 percent said they waste at least an hour a day because of distractions brought on by these tools.

Other non-work distractions, such as time spent on office pools for the March Madness college basketball tournament, shopping, and watching cat videos, also contribute to technology-related non-productive work time.

Consideration:

Using technology can be both helpful and fun. Thus, it is no surprise why workers take advantage of their access to technology in the workplace (including the home-office workplace) to perform some non-work-related activities. A recommendation that I have made to workers in this situation is an off-shoot of a recommendation I received many years ago from a professional bodybuilder. At the time, I was working out and dieting in hopes of getting into the best physical shape possible. The bodybuilder overheard a friend and me talking about our struggles to maintain diet-discipline and fight the temptation of junk food. The bodybuilder suggested the following: If you deny yourself the (junk) foods that you enjoy, the temptation becomes so great that it is inevitable you will "cheat." And, once you do, it'll be hard to stop. He recommended that, every other weekend – pick a day, Saturday or Sunday – we should allow ourselves to eat anything that we wanted. By doing this, he argued, it would lessen our temptation to cheat throughout the week and make it easier for us to maintain diet-discipline; it worked!

Based on that bodybuilder's input, my recommendation is this: if it is hard for you to focus on getting your most important work done because of the temptation of Facebook, for example, then place two 15-minute blocks of time on your calendar each day to do non-work-related computer and Internet stuff (within your organization's guidelines). By doing so, you will know that you have allocated time on your calendar for social media activity, and you will feel less urgency to cheat with this activity during the work day.

Workers to whom I have offered this recommendation report two interesting results: their temptation to engage with social media, etc. throughout the day has been greatly diminished, and they have found that they do not even use the full half-hour of time they have allocated for these activities.

3. Constant Connectivity

"Constant connectivity" means that, during the workday, you are always connected to the Internet and are, therefore, reachable and available for contact. When you are in the office, you are available for in-person communication and you are reachable by email, desk phone, mobile phone, text message, instant-message, video conferencing, and/or intercom. When you are away from your workplace, you are reachable by all of the above with the exception of in-person communication and your desk phone. In other words, you are *constantly* available as long as you have a device or phone that is *connected* to a network.

There are productivity-related challenges when workers are constantly connected. For starters, constantly-connected workers are expected to be reachable and available throughout the workday, whether they are working outside the office or not. In some cases, employees are expected to be reachable after hours, on weekends, and while on vacation. When people know that workers are reachable at any time of the day because they have an organization-issued mobile phone (which also contains email, text, messaging, and video conferencing), for example, people will contact the employee at all hours of the day. And when the worker is connected, the result will often be an assignment added to his or her to-do list, a distraction, or the interruption of something important that he or she was already completing. Each time a worker is interrupted, the result is a loss of productivity time. It is not uncommon for workers to waste as much as 5 hours of their work day managing interruptions and re-starting work in which they were engaged prior to being interrupted.

Consideration:

- Validate connectivity expectations. Consider asking your manager to establish his or her expectations regarding such things as how quickly you should respond to email messages and what is the best method of communication if your boss needs something urgently.

- Set connectivity limits. Some organizations have e-mail-free zones in which no one is allowed to read or check email during certain hours of the day. Other companies have imposed policies which prohibit workers from holding on-site, in-person meetings between 8AM and 4PM. Or, simply set your own boundaries around when you will be disconnected.

- Use an orange cone. Modern office spaces are increasingly being designed with open floor plans. This means there are no cubicles for worker privacy. Open floor plans lead to workers being interrupted by others. If you are busy and want to complete an assignment without Bill walking up to your desk to discuss last night's baseball game, try placing an orange cone (or any brightly colored object) on your desk as a sign that you are not to be disturbed. People will see the cone on your desk and know that it is equivalent to a "Do Not Disturb" sign.

- Turn off your phone. When you are working on something important, turn off your phone to avoid phone interruptions.

- Turn off email notifications. If your job function is something other than Executive Administrator or a direct report to a senior executive, try turning off your pop-up email notifications to reduce being distracted by every new email message that is sent to you. If you are uncomfortable about turning off your email notifications for fear that you might miss something urgent or something from your boss, then, depending on the email service you use, you can create email "rules" that will allow you to be notified by pop-up message or sound whenever you receive an email that meets your acceptance criteria, such as an email from your boss or a family member.

- Decline valueless meetings. Let's face it, not all meetings and conference calls that we attend are worthwhile. In fact, many are down-right useless. Every time we attend one of these meetings or conference calls of questionable value, we waste valuable time that otherwise could have been spent more productively. The suggestion? Just say "No." When you receive a meeting invitation and scan the agenda, if the meeting's agenda does not relate to something important that you must achieve, then you should make a decision as to whether or not the meeting is worth attending. If you decide that it is not, then decline it or discuss your participation with the meeting organizer.

4. Noise

Noise levels in offices – particularly offices with open floor plans – create significant distractions for workers. Other than requesting that the organization place noise-cancelling tiles on the walls, consider using noise-cancelling headphones or listen to music through these devices.

....

Recommendations for working productively:

- **Prioritize** activities, tasks, and to-dos. If I could only recommend one practice that would have the greatest impact on worker productivity it would be this: prioritize all activities, tasks, and to-dos on your list by asking of each: If I complete this task, will its completion get me one step closer to achieving (at least) one of my objectives. If the answer is yes, then the task is considered important and necessary. If the answer is no, then it likely is not.

- Reduce "busy work" and eliminate "brownie work."

- Cut down on productivity detractors, such as interruptions, constant connectivity, and the non-work-related use of technology. Establish protocols and guidelines with your manager and team members about how you will work together and become more productive.

STEP 7: BE DILIGENT

To be diligent at work is to perform your activities with a measure of determination, care, and consideration. It is also about having the perseverance to ensure that a job is done well.

One of the most causal-yet-under-acknowledged factors impacting workers' job success is the degree of diligence with which they perform their jobs. From a practical standpoint, work diligence can be comprised of anything impactful, from competing work assignments to quickly identifying problems. Two contributors to worker diligence that are highly-impactful, yet easy to address, are *following instructions* and *being responsible.*

Following instructions seems like a no-brainer for workers: you listen (really *listen*) to the things that are being asked, you write them down or capture them electronically in a place where you can easily retrieve them as needed, you validate that you have captured the instructions accurately, you ask questions for clarification, and you complete the tasks as instructed. If you are unable to perform an activity, you can then ask for help and/or get trained on how to do it so that you can complete the activity as instructed.

What hurts workers' job performance, especially in the eyes of a manager, is when the manager (or other co-workers) gives clear, specific instructions on what needs to be done and by when, and the worker achieves neither objective.

Think RACI

Within Project Management circles, project leaders follow a process of charting the responsibilities of those with a role in some aspect of the project as a way to clarify roles and expectations. This role and responsibility charting is referred to as the RACI responsibility matrix.

RACI identifies project participants based on the role they will play, the function they will serve, the communication channel they will follow, and/or that which is expected of them to deliver a project or business process. The roles identified through the RACI process generally include:

- **R– Responsible**: Those who are required to do the work to complete an assignment or task; the "doers."

- **A– Accountable**: The final authority. The one ultimately answerable for the successful completion of the deliverable, and the one who delegates the work to those *responsible*.

- **C– Consulted**: Subject matter experts or authorities whose input is sought for the successful delivery of an initiative.

- **I– Informed**: Those who must be informed about an initiative's progress and status.

When it comes to diligence, the performance of the first two roles listed – those who are *responsible* and those who are *accountable* – has the greatest impact on a worker's job success. If you are responsible for completing an assignment with the degree of completeness and quality expected, and you fail to do so, your failure may impact an important project, a client, a team's performance, and even the organization's performance.

Suppose that you work for a shoe manufacturer, and your job is that of a *Cutter*. You are responsible for cutting the shoe's leather into the shape required for its design. As a cutter, you are also responsible for precisely cutting 100 leather uppers each day so that the company can meet its daily sales order quantity. There are seven fundamental steps in the shoe-making process. The steps that follow the *cutting* stage are: stitching, lasting, sole stitching, edge trimming, finishing, and quality check. Since your job, cutting, is a prerequisite for these other stages of the shoe-making process, if you do not perform your job effectively and deliver fewer than the required 100 leather uppers per day, then no one else can do their jobs, and the company will not be able to meet its 100-pair daily order quota.

By not being *responsible* for the requirements and expectations of your job (i.e. doing your job poorly), when it comes time for your performance review and assessment, your job performance will be considered unsuccessful. In addition, your manager – the person who is ultimately *ac-*

countable for the shoe department's output – will also be rated poorly on his or her performance assessment (due in large part to your job performance).

This example of the accountable manager illustrates another important aspect of productivity (in this case, *producing* 100 pairs of shoes daily): **the manager and the worker share responsibility for each other's success**. Therefore, it should be mandatory that the manager is fully vested and engaged in the worker's performance and job success.

> The manager and the worker share responsibility for each other's success. Therefore, it should be mandatory that the manager is fully vested and engaged in the worker's performance and job success.

Being responsible is about having an obligation to do something as expected and as determined by those who define the standards and expectations for that which must be done. To fail at fulfilling that obligation – assuming it is realistic, fair, achievable, and supported – is to be irresponsible and unsuccessful in one's job.

Recommendations for being diligent in your job:

- Listen intently and follow instructions. Capture the validated (by you) instructions and tasks in a place where you can retrieve them easily when needed. I recommend you use an electronic tool that allows for retrieval anywhere, such as: todoist, Evernote, TaskTask, Microsoft Outlook, 2Do, Google Docs, ToDo.txt, reminder apps, or even document creation software. The list of options is endless.

- Hold yourself responsible and accountable for performing your job and its associated activities as defined. If you find that you cannot effectively perform an activity, then seek help and ask to be trained or coached on how to do the work.

- If you are a manager who is accountable to a team or an initiative, jointly plan with your workers to ensure their success at diligently performing activities and being responsible; your success is likely interconnected with theirs. Hold periodic check-in reviews so that, if you find there is a challenge with the worker completing an assignment, you can provide the support and resources necessary to reverse that course.

- Remember: Since you are ultimately accountable for doing your job successfully, whenever there is an obstacle, impediment, or problem that arises that negatively impacts your ability to be as successful as possible with the greatest degree of efficiency, take responsibility for the problem. Blaming others for things that you are accountable for is irresponsible and non-productive. Be a leader. Take responsibility. Chart a new course to get back on track with your own success.

STEP 8: CONSTANTLY WORK TO IMPROVE YOUR SKILLS AND ABILITY

Upgrading your skills and capabilities is an obvious endeavor if you have discovered a job-skill gap between your abilities and your job duties and responsibilities. However, workers should strive to continually upgrade their level of knowledge, skills, experience, and job acumen if they want to remain viable in their current role or become a candidate for a future role.

Things change. Remember the *Switchboard Operator?*

Job requirements change, just as – in the case of both for-profit and not-for-profit businesses – the "needs of the business" change. The *needs of the business* is a broad term used by organizational leaders to explain, rationalize, or justify usually significant changes that are to take place within an organization. Suppose that a business' stakeholders decide (demand) that the business must improve its profit margins. One of the ways business leaders have identified to improve margins is by reassigning workers into different roles that are needed to adapt to changes in the market in which they operate. In this case, the *needs of the business* dictate that some workers will need to be redeployed into other roles, others will need to be retrained, and some, for whom there is no longer a role within the company, may have to be displaced.

In this example, those workers who have the skills necessary to adapt to changing market conditions will be best positioned to not only remain employed by the organization, but will also be well-positioned to successfully perform their job.

The reality is that most workers' skills gradually decline over a period of months or years. So, keeping your skills current is one of the most important things you can do to succeed in your job, to be prepared for changes due to the *needs of the business*, and to prepare for new opportunities. It is worth noting that worker development and training is a partnership between the organization and the worker; it is not the manager's or the organization's sole responsibility to ensure that its workers' skills remain current. The worker shares an equal – if not greater – responsibility for their own development and professional growth.

Identify and Close Job- and Market-Skill Gaps

A "market-skill gap" is the difference between a worker's current skills, knowledge, and capability levels, and the skills, knowledge, and capabilities that market shifts (often brought on by technological advances and competition) dictate a worker must possess to remain viable in a certain job role.

Job-skill gaps and market-skill gaps can both be assessed in a similar manner.

1. Take inventory of your current skills, knowledge, and ability levels.

2. Identify and document the skills, knowledge, and capabilities that are required to do your job at present, and that will be required moving forward (over the next 12 to 24 months).

3. Map the two and identify the gaps between your current skills, knowledge, and ability, and those required for the job.

Job- and Work-Skill Map

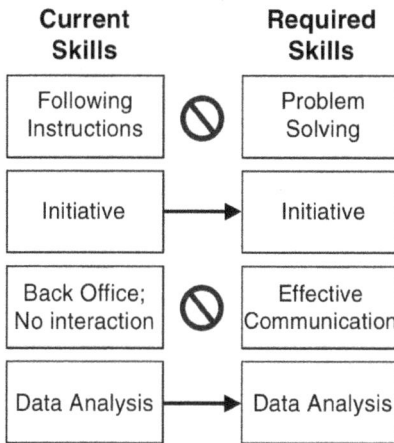

Current Skills		Required Skills
Following Instructions	🚫	Problem Solving
Initiative	→	Initiative
Back Office; No interaction	🚫	Effective Communication
Data Analysis	→	Data Analysis

This mapping reveals that the worker must improve his or her problem solving and effective communication skills if the worker is to be successful in the job currently and in the near-term.

After your job- and market-skill gaps have been identified, work with your manager, the Learning and Development team, mentors, other successful workers, and any other relevant parties to develop a training and development plan to get you where you need to be. The plan that is developed should be documented, agreed upon by you and your manager, funded, and added to your annual development plan that is part of your performance plan. It is also a good idea to establish periodic check-ins with your manager to review your learning and development plan, and to ensure that your development goals are on-track.

The Benefits of Job-Skill Improvement

There are many benefits workers receive from learning new things and maintaining and improving their skills and ability levels. These benefits may include:

- Better job performance, leading to enrichment and work engagement. This helps make workers happier and more satisfied at work.

- Marketability. If the worker is compelled to seek another job within or outside their current organization, better skills, knowledge, and ability can make the worker a more attractive candidate for other positions.

- Self-confidence. The more skills, knowledge, and experience we acquire, and the more we understand relevant issues, the more we acquire an added degree of confidence that we can perform any task we are charged with performing. When we are confident in our abilities, we believe that we can do anything, and we will work to do just that – even if it requires figuring out how to do some things. This contributes to job success.

- Increased productivity. As you become more skilled and capable, you become better at doing your job. The better you become at performing the activities, tasks, and to-dos required of your job, the more productive you will become. This improves your odds of job success.

- Better support for your co-workers and team. When you are more knowledgeable, your peers can benefit from your knowledge. This will help them perform their jobs more successfully, too. When this occurs, the team and the organization benefit from your and their success.

Recommendations for improving your skills and ability:

- Take responsibility for upgrading your job-skill development and growth. While your manager and organization have a vested interest in your growth and development, you must become the catalyst for it to come to fruition.

- Create a job- and market-skill map between your current skills, knowledge, and ability levels, and identify and close any existing job- and market-skill gaps.

- Work with your manager, the Learning and Development team, mentors, other successful workers, and any other relevant parties to develop a training and development plan to get you from where you are today to where you need to be in the near-term.

- Establish periodic development and growth check-ins with your manager to review your learning and development plan, and to ensure that your development goals are on-track to being realized.

- Read: If you have a library card, one of the easiest ways to gain knowledge and make improvements is by reading. Your organization cannot afford or is unwilling to fund a training class you want to take? Read a book. Can't read? Then get the audio-book version. Reading reduces stress and improves memory, so anytime you can supplement your development efforts with reading or listen to books, you will benefit in myriad ways.

STEP 9: ESTABLISH RECURRING MEETINGS WITH YOUR MANAGER

Establishing open lines of communication between the worker and manager goes a long way toward improving the worker-manager relationship. As I wrote previously, *The Wall Street Journal* shared that actively engaged workers believe they can approach their manager with any type of question; this is a testament to the worker-manager relationship and the openness of communication between the two parties.

To enable and facilitate the ability of the manager to provide coaching, direction, leadership, decision-making, guidance, updates, training and development follow-up, and apply the previously-discussed *direct manager levers* to the worker-manager relationship, a regularly-recurring scheduled meeting should be established and added to both parties' calendars. It is also an opportunity for the worker to get to know the manager better and to keep the manager informed about their satisfaction, work progress, and anything else of importance. And, if nothing else, this regularly-recurring meeting or call will force the worker and manager to talk about … *something*. A conversation about *anything* is better than not conversing and communicating at all.

If, for example, the manager-worker meeting or call is scheduled weekly, then I recommend that, throughout the week, the worker and manager write down potential topics to discuss with each other. And, on the day of the meeting, each person should collect their discussion topics and use these topics as the agenda for the meeting or call.

Recommendations:

- Institute a regularly-recurring scheduled meeting or phone call between you and your boss, and add the meeting or call to both parties' calendars.

- Throughout the week, you and your manager should note potential topics to discuss with each other during your recurring meeting or call. On the day of the meeting or call, each of you should collect your discussion topics, compile them, and use these topics as the agenda for the meeting or call.

STEP 10: REWARD YOURSELF!

Reward yourself for making progress toward your goals and objectives. For example, after you have completed an important activity, a milestone, or a critical success factor, give yourself a small reward. While small, these rewards motivate you to continue what can at times be a challenging effort to achieve job-success.

Progress at work is important for many reasons, some of which have already been discussed throughout this book. One benefit of progressing toward your goals and objectives that has not been discussed is the good feeling we get when we complete an important activity.

Without getting too deep into the scientific weeds, when our brain recognizes that something significant is about to happen, it triggers the release of *dopamine*. Dopamine is a neurotransmitter (a chemical messenger, of sorts) that helps control the brain's reward and pleasure centers. It also enables us not only to see an opportunity for rewards, but also to undertake action to move toward them. Put differently, when your brain recognizes that something good or bad is about to happen, dopamine kicks in, encouraging us to either act on the good thing or to avoid the bad thing.

When our brain recognizes that we are about to complete an important action item or critical success factor, dopamine kicks in and gives us a sense of pleasure. This encourages us to move forward with completing the activity; completing important activities gives us a reward in the form of a sense of pleasure. This reward then serves as a *motivating factor*, encouraging us to work diligently to complete additional important activities to continue to receive the dopamine-induced reward.

It is also important for workers to reward *themselves* for a job well done. A piece of chocolate, a slice of pizza, a new pair of shoes, a mid-day nap, a walk in the park, a massage, a ticket to a sporting event, or watching a movie, any reward that provides you with pleasure will suffice. Whether it is for completing important activities or CSFs, giving yourself a reward for completing a milestone – no matter how small, as long as it is significant or important – is something that you can do proactively, of your own accord, to continue to motivate yourself to complete important work activities and reach key milestones.

Recommendations:

- Reward yourself for completing important activities, tasks, to-dos, initiatives, projects, and CSFs, and also for achieving important milestones, goals, and objectives.

- Create a list of rewards or things that bring you pleasure – even guilty pleasures. Each time you complete a reward-worthy activity (as determined by you alone), treat yourself to one of the items on your reward list.

8

CHAPTER**EGT**

A SUMMARY OF THE RECOMMENDATIONS
TOWARD DOING YOUR JOB SUCCESSFULLY

SUMMARY: A 10-STEP PROCESS
TOWARD DOING YOUR JOB SUCCESSFULLY

STEP 1: Understand what your job *really* is

Recommendations

- Understand the true purpose of your job. What were you really hired to do?

- Complete this sentence: If I do my job successfully, then the value that I will provide to this organization is

  _____.

- Map your skills and experience against job responsibilities and identify gaps.

- Understand whether or not you would be successful in the job if you *only* executed (successfully) the job requirements as stated. If you determine that you cannot be successful by doing so, then use the valuable experiences of your predecessors and your boss to understand what *really* is needed to do the job successfully.

- Speak with your predecessors in the role who have successfully performed the job and note best practices and recommendations. Also, learn from the mistakes of those who have performed the job unsuccessfully. Add this insight into your job success plan.

STEP 2: Carry out an honest inventory of your current state and perform a gap analysis

Recommendation

- Perform a gap analysis.

- Document a comprehensive list of the job duties and responsibilities you are charged with performing this year.

- Take an honest inventory of your talent, ability, and skills as they relate to your ability to successfully perform your job responsibilities.

- Identify and document the gaps that exist between the job duties and your capability to perform them. Put differently, identify the job duties and responsibilities that you cannot successfully perform.

- Determine what is needed for you to close the TAS-gaps and successfully perform the job duties.

- Document what is needed and, working with your manager, develop an actionable learning and development plan that will enable you to acquire the skills and knowledge that are necessary for you to successfully perform your job duties and responsibilities.

STEP 3: Ensure that the objectives you are charged with achieving to have a successful year are S.M.A.R.T.

Recommendations

- Do not sign off on or approve a performance plan if the work objectives that you are charged with achieving are not S.M.A.R.T. Recommend that your boss (and even Human Resources, as appropriate) agree to work and collaborate with you on crafting objectives that you understand, are aligned with, and agree to.

- For each objective, ask three critical questions: (1) "How much and by when," to help quantify them and define the time parameter; (2) "Is every parameter clearly defined and specific?" If not, clarify and specify them; and (3) "Is the objective S.M.A.R.T.?" These questions should also be asked of other performance criteria, including: "Behavioral" Goals, Performance Competencies, Duties, Success Criteria, and other desired outcomes contained within a typical performance plan.

- To improve productivity and achieve higher success rates more quickly, identify the important, priority activities on which you should spend your time. To do this, each day compile a list of your tasks and to-dos. Then, from that list, determine those activities that are priorities by asking of each activity, "If I complete this activity, will it get me one step closer to achieving a goal or objective?" If the answer is yes, then the activity is important; if the answer is no, then you will have to determine whether or not it is worth completing.

Another question you can ask to help you determine which activities are most important, requiring that they be completed most quickly, is "What would be the consequences if I do not do this activity now or today?" Those activities with the most significant consequences – either good or bad – are priorities; complete them first. By prioritizing your activities, tasks, and to-dos to focus on completing the most important items, you will then have the ability to track your progress toward achieving your objectives. For each important activity you complete, you should get a step closer to achieving these objectives, and – because the objectives should now be measurable – you can track your progress based on the number of completed activities.

After you have determined which of your listed activities are important and/or priorities, place them on your calendar to ensure that you allocate time to get them done. There is a significantly-greater likelihood that you will actually do something if you put that activity on your calendar.

STEP 4: Document your goals and objectives and make them visible; review them daily

Recommendations

- Ensure that your goals are clearly articulated and your objectives are clearly defined and S.M.A.R.T.;

- Document your goals/objectives so that they are captured and can be stored and retrieved;

- Place a copy of the goals/objectives in a place that you can see them at least once per day. Some people place them on their bathroom mirror. Some people place them on their computer and phone as their start-up screens, and others put them in places like the front cover of their notebooks.

- Use your goals and objectives to qualify your daily list of activities, tasks, and to-dos and determine which are important; in other words, what are your priorities. Do this by asking this question about each activity: If I complete this activity, will it get me closer to accomplishing my goal or achieving my objective?

STEP 5: Develop a plan for how you will achieve a "make"

Recommandations

- Develop a plan to "show a make:" Create a job-success plan that outlines how you will achieve your job-related work objectives. Having work objectives is pointless if you are not serious about achieving them. If you are, however, serious then you must determine how you can do it. This plan should include your work objectives, the initiatives / projects that must be completed to achieve these objectives, and the tasks that must be completed to accomplish the initiatives.

- Use the *Job-Success Plan Workbook*: To facilitate your job-success planning efforts, I have provided a workbook that takes you step-by-step through the entire plan-creation process. The workbook and all the necessary forms are provided in the Appendix, and a downloadable, full-size version of the workbook is available at the website, www.TabEdwards.com

- Identify Critical Success Factors / Initiatives: Initiatives identify and define the undertakings that must often be fulfilled for objectives to be realized. Initiatives are often considered to be *critical success factors*. Critical success factors (CSFs) are activities that must absolutely be completed for a worker to achieve her or his objectives.

CSFs/Initiatives can be identified by asking this three-pronged question:

(1) What are the major activities or *things* that must be completed to reach this objective?

(2) If I complete all these activities or *things*, will I reach the objective?" (If the answer is "no," then you must add different or additional potential initiatives until the answer – based on your learned belief, which may include the supporting opinion of others – is "yes")

(3) If I do not complete a specific activity or thing, will I still be successful in achieving my objectives? If the answer is "no," then it is likely a well-defined initiative. If the answer is "yes," then that activity is probably not necessary for you to spend time completing.

- Apply "If-Then" Logic: Ensure that cause-and-effect logic is built into your "make" plan, such that completing your important action items, tasks, and to-dos will result in completed initiatives or projects, and completed initiatives/projects will result in the achievement of your objectives.

- **Adjust**: Review the plan daily (or at the least weekly) and adjust the plan, as necessary, based on new learnings, obstacles, delays, or other factors that impact the successful completion of your initiatives and/or the achievement of your objectives.

STEP 6: Work productively

Recommendations for working productively

- **Prioritize** activities, tasks, and to-dos. If I could only recommend one practice that would have the greatest impact on worker productivity, it would be this: prioritize the activities, tasks, and to-dos on your list by asking of each: If I complete this task will its completion get me one step closer to achieving one of my objectives? If the answer is "yes," then the task is considered important and necessary. If the answer is "no," then it likely is not.

- Reduce "busy work" and eliminate "brownie work."

- Reduce and eliminate productivity detractors.

STEP 7: Be diligent

Recommendations for being diligent in your job include

- Listen intently and follow instructions. Capture the validated (by you) instructions and tasks in a place where you can easily retrieve them when needed. I recommend you use an electronic tool that allows for retrieval anywhere, such as todoist, Evernote, TaskTask, Microsoft Outlook, 2Do, Google Docs, ToDo.txt, reminder apps, or even document creation software (to name just a few options).

- Hold yourself responsible for performing your job and its associated activities, as defined. If you find that you cannot effectively perform an activity, then seek help and ask to be trained or coached on how to do it.

- If you are a manager who is accountable to a team or an initiative, jointly plan with your fellow workers on how to ensure their success by diligently performing activities and being responsible; your success is likely intertwined with theirs. Hold periodic check-in reviews so that, if you find there is a challenge with the worker completing an assignment, you can provide the support and resources necessary to reverse that course.

- Remember: Since you are ultimately accountable for doing your job successfully, whenever there is an obstacle, impediment, or problem that arises that negatively impacts your ability to be as successful as possible with the greatest degree of efficiency, take responsibility for the problem. Blaming others is irresponsible and non-productive. Be a leader. Take responsibility. Chart a new way to get back on-course toward your own success.

STEP 8: Constantly work to improve your skills and ability

Recommendations for improving your skills and ability

- Take responsibility for upgrading your job skill development and growth. While your manager and the organization each have a vested interest in your growth and development, you must become the catalyst for driving it to fruition.

- Create a job- and market-skill map between your current skills, knowledge, and ability levels, and identify and close any existing job- and market-skill gaps.

- Work with your manager, the Learning and Development team, mentors, other successful workers, and any other relevant parties to develop a training and development plan to get you from where you are today to where you need to be in the near-term.

- Establish periodic development and growth check-ins with your manager to review your learning and development plan, and to ensure that your development goals are on-track to being realized.

- Read: If you have a library card, one of the easiest ways to gain knowledge and improve your skills is by reading. Your organization cannot afford or is unwilling to fund a training class you want to take? Read a book. Can't read? Then get the audio-book version. Reading reduces stress and improves memory, so anytime you can supplement your development efforts by reading or listening to books, you will benefit in myriad ways.

STEP 9: Establish recurring meetings with your manager

Recommendations

- Institute a regularly-recurring scheduled meeting or phone call between you and your boss, and add the meeting or call to both parties' calendars.

- Throughout the week, you and your manager should note potential topics to discuss with each other during your recurring meeting or call. On the day of the meeting or call, each of you should collect these discussion topics, compile them, and use the topics as the agenda for the meeting or call.

STEP 10: Reward yourself!

Recommendations

- Reward yourself for completing important activities, tasks, to-dos, initiatives, projects, and CSFs, as well as for achieving important milestones, goals, and objectives.

- Create a list of rewards or things that bring you pleasure – even guilty pleasures. Each time you complete a reward-worthy activity (as determined by you alone), treat yourself to an item on your reward list.

CONCLUSION

YOU ARE ACCOUNTABLE
FOR YOUR *OWN* JOB-SUCCESS

QUESTION: If you perform your job unsuccessfully year-in and year-out, who will most likely be separated from their job, you or your manager? The answer is obvious: you.

If the answer to this question was factually "both my manager *and* I would be fired," then you could argue that the responsibility for your job success was a 50-50 proposition: 50% your responsibility and 50% your boss's responsibility. But, it's not.

While genuine uncertainty remains about what managers do for their organizations, the activities in which an organization engages are determined, traditionally, by some form of a manager. Managers serve a special function within organizations and have the responsibility of making decisions and executing plans – ensuring that goals and objectives are achieved.

In support of plan execution, managers develop and manage people, which means, to some extent, managers are ultimately held responsible for their subordinates' decisions and activities. Why? Because – in terms of the RACI responsibility matrix – the manager is ultimately held *accountable* for the organization's success, but the subordinate is *responsible* for executing the specific requirements of his or her job, and is *accountable* for his or her *own* job success. The subordinate's success is a prerequisite for the manager's success; if the subordinate fails at his or her job, then the manager would find it challenging to successfully perform his or her own job. So, as history tells us, if a manager believes that the subordinate is incapable of performing his or her job successfully – therefore negatively impacting the manager's performance – the manager will replace the subordinate with a worker whom the manager believes *can* do the job. The result: the manager stays and the subordinate goes.

Even though the manager is not wholly responsible for the worker's job success, the manager is complicit in the worker's job failure because, as previously stated: *In support of execution, managers develop and manage people, which means, to some extent, managers are ultimately held responsible for their subordinates' decisions and activities.* Although the manager's share of the blame might not generally be as high as 50%, they do share responsibility for a worker's *success*, in part, because it is in their best interest to do so.

Being successful in your job is about being an active participant, rather than a bystander, in your own success. You cannot, nor should you, expect someone else to be responsible for *your* job success. Many stakeholders within an organization share some responsibility for ensuring that a worker, who was hired by a collective within the organization – the manager, human resources representatives, learning and development's on-boarding team, the worker's team members, and other associates – succeeds. Thus, I will concede that the worker is not 100% responsible for his or her own success. However, the worker holds the lion's-share of responsibility. When it comes to understanding who has responsibility for a worker's job success and to what degree, I developed the *70-20-9-1 Rule*, which is spelled out in greater detail below.

THE 70-20-9-1 RULE

The worker is 70% responsible for his or her job success. It is not 100%, because a manager's job is partly to support and contribute to worker success. The cast of people who helped bring the worker into the organization shares responsibility, too. Remember: one of the main reasons why workers fail in their jobs is because they were a bad-hire in the first place.

Why 70%? Over the course of my career managing teams and leading people, whether it was as a Principal at a boutique consulting firm or as the leader of a $2.6 billion *Fortune* Top 20 corporation, there was one inescapable truism when it came to a manager's impact on a worker's performance: managers set strategies, allocate resources, make decisions, and provide guidance that all impact whether or not a manager's direct-reports succeed in their jobs. If you list each such element and compare the number of success-impacting elements controlled by the manager against the number of success-impacting elements controlled by the worker, and you weight them according to their relative impact on a worker's job success, you will find that approximately 20% of a manager's responsibilities directly impact a worker's job success. On the other hand, 70% of weighted elements are directly controlled and influenced by the worker. As a consultant, I have performed these analyses many times over the years in the course of conducting performance-improvement engagements. Surprisingly, in these analyses, the balance between worker and manager job-impacting responsibilities has remained consistent.

What's interesting to note is that other people, in addition to the worker and manager, also make decisions that impact workers' job success. For that reason, they too bear some responsibility for ensuring a successful workforce. Human resources representatives, learning and development on-boarding teams, the worker's fellow team members, and other associates within the organization can and do make decisions that impact a worker's ability to succeed in his or her job. Though their contribution to a worker's job success is collectively less than that of the manager – by at least half, I have found – they still can have a significant impact.

I will acknowledge that The 70-20-9-1 Rule is not totally scientific and is mostly based on the real-world experiences and estimations from consulting studies and engagements conducted by me and other consultants with whom I have worked over the past 25 years. That said, when conducting performance improvement engagements for individuals within organizations, these allocations of responsibility have held up rather well over time.

Based on this assessment data, performance improvement studies, surveys, interviews, data analysis, and other information sources that have provided my consulting colleagues and me with insight over the years, I have determined that, while the worker is 100% *accountable* for his or her job success, the worker is only approximately 70% *responsible* for his or her own job success. I also concluded that the manager is approximately 20% responsible, and other associates and functional area representatives are roughly 9% responsible. The remaining 1%? Luck. To quote author and journalist Hunter S. Thompson, "Luck is a very thin wire between survival and disaster."

Contribution to Workers' Job Success

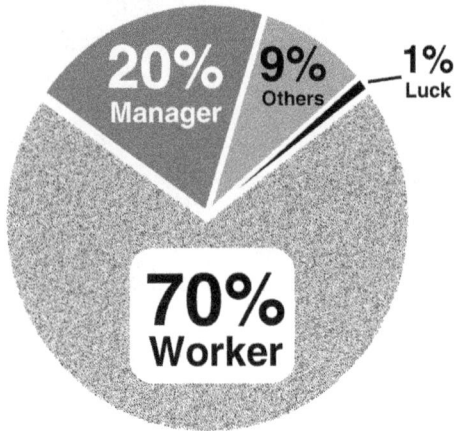

20% Manager

9% Others

1% Luck

70% Worker

Yes, the worker is ultimately accountable for his or her own success. However, the reality is that **it takes an organization**. If the organization pays you a fair wage, then you have an obligation to fulfill the job requirements they pay you to perform. If the manager has agreed to have the worker become a member of his or her team, the manager has an obligation to help the worker succeed in the job to help the team and the organization. If the human resources recruiter approved the then-candidate-worker to pass the recruitment and hiring process, then they will have an obligation to ensure that the worker is best positioned to succeed based on the worker's skills, experience, knowledge, and ability compared with general job qualifications. If the Learning and Development team is responsible for increasing individual knowledge and raising competency levels in activities, tasks, and to-dos determined in the worker's job profile, then they have an obligation to ensure that they can support a worker's job proficiency.

Who knows? With all of this, and a little luck, then you could be well on your way to achieving job, career, and life success.

ABOUT THE AUTHOR

TAB EDWARDS is a thought-leading business services consultant, best-selling author, speaker, and educator who works with business and organization leaders globally to help them make better, more informed decisions, convert those decisions into actions, and deliver sustainable success. His principles have been adopted by organizations around the globe, and his best- practices have been implemented by firms of every type, including global enterprises, corporations, SMBs, start-ups, public sector organizations, universities, and non-profits. His workshops, coaching sessions, seminars, and speaking engagements are highly-regarded and have been delivered to general audiences and professionals at organizations, big and small.

He is the author of ten books and is a globally-recognized critical thinker with expertise in performance improvement, business-unit level strategy and execution, and sales optimization. He has worked with thousands of individuals and organizations, helping them become more effective at accomplishing their goals and being better at their pursuits (whatever they may be).

Edwards has held global consulting and leadership positions at some of the world's most admired companies, including: IBM Corporation, General Electric, AmerisourceBergen, and Hewlett-Packard, where he achieved the position of Master-Level Consultant.

TAB EDWARDS ENGAGEMENTS

FREE 1-HOUR SEMINAR OR KEYNOTE ADDRESS!

Tab Edwards is available to deliver a free 1-hour seminar or keynote address on-site at an organization's designated location (certain qualifications apply). Topics covered include:

- **Toward Job-Success:** A 3-step process toward achieving professional success;
- **Mutual Success at Work:** A collaboration between the individual contributor and manager;
- **The Performance Plan:** Does your Performance Plan contribute to job-failure or enable job-success;
- **Toward Sales Optimization**: A discussion of overall sales improvement and sales professionals' success;
- **Job-Performance:** Why we fail and why we succeed, and what we can do about this.

For additional information and to request a free 1-hour engagement, please visit us on the web at: www.TabEdwards.com

SPEAKING ENGAGEMENTS AND WORKSHOPS

Tab Edwards is available to work with leaders and organizations in various capacities, including:

SPEAKING ENGAGEMENTS

Whether inspiring audiences, motivating teams, or delivering keynote addresses, Tab is prepared to deliver information that will motivate your team to higher performance levels and provide them with useful information, doing so in an entertaining, engaging, and uplifting manner.

JOB-SUCCESS WORKSHOPS

Tab starts this workshop by validating and ensuring alignment between the organization's, business units', management's, and individuals' goals and objectives – down to the performance plan level; the unfortunate reality is that, in most organizations, this link and alignment are not in place. And, until they are in place, workers will struggle to be as successful in their jobs as they could be.

Tab continues by working with stakeholders to assess the root causes of underperformance, identify gaps between workers' capabilities and job requirements, and develop individual and joint plans between individual contributors and managers to ensure a higher degree of success at achieving job-related work goals and objectives.

COACHING WORKSHOPS

Tab has worked with organization leaders, managers, and individual contributors globally on how to become more effective in their jobs and given areas of responsibility. He also works with professionals on upgrading their overall performance level and effectiveness across various functional areas.

His customizable team and individual coaching workshop topics have included:

- Individual and team goal-attainment;
- Sales optimization and team effectiveness;
- Management coaching and strategy proficiency;
- Team growth and development;
- Business-unit-level and team-based strategy and strategy execution; and
- Effective presentation skills, public speaking, and communication.

BUSINESS PROCESS IMPROVEMENT WORKSHOPS

By providing organizations with a clear benchmark of their current performance and issues impeding progress and goal-attainment, Tab and his professional team work with organizations to identify areas of inefficiency, underperformance, and high cost, and to define improvement solutions. The aim is to reduce costs, improve efficiency, upgrade performance, and deliver a sustainable competitive advantage.

STRATEGY WORKSHOPS

The Water Performance Academy's team of experts can work with your organization on every aspect of business-unit-level strategy, including planning sessions, workgroup discussions, current-strategy analysis, strategy development workshops, strategy scorecarding, strategy execution engagement, and strategy coaching and guidance.

For more information on these or any other support services provided by Tab Edwards, please contact us at 856.248.0706, or by email at Info@TabEdwards.com
Follow Tab on Twitter: **@TabAuthor**

DOING
YOUR JOB
THE WORKSHOP

This HALF-, FULL-, or 2-Day Workshop includes pre-workshop planning & analysis, and is designed for managers and their associates with an interest in: improving the manager-associate relationship; improving performance; and increasing the odds of job-success.

THE MODULES INCLUDE

PRE-WORKSHOP

- Pre-Workshop Planning: Define the desired outcomes
- Pre-Workshop Assessment: Understand the Current State
- Pre-Workshop Gap-Analyses (Part 1)

IN-WORKSHOP

- What is "Job-Success"?
- The Anatomy of Job Success
- Why workers succeed and fail in their jobs: An exploration
- Team or individual working session: Ensuring well-defined goals
- Job- and TAS-Gap Analyses (Part 2)
- Developing Your Job-Success Plan
- More!

For more information, contact us at Info@ TabEdwards.com

WORK WITH A
PURPOSE

APPENDIX

THE
JOB-SUCCESS
PLAN
WORKBOOK

This *Job-Success Plan Workbook* should be used in conjunction with the "10-Step Process Toward Doing Your Job Successfully" that has been outlined above.

I recommend that the forms in this section be reproduced in a spreadsheet or other document, or photocopied and, ideally, enlarged so that they are easier for you to use as you develop your job-success plan. A full-size workbook is available for free and can be downloaded directly from the website, www.TabEdwards.com.

INSTRUCTIONS

1. Reproduce or photocopy the forms in this section, or download the *Job-Success Plan Workbook* from our website.

2. Follow all instructions, answer each question, and write your answers in the appropriate box or section on the correct form.

3. When and where relevant, seek input and help from your manager, co-workers, and other stakeholders to help you craft the best, most realistic, and impactful plan possible.

4. Using the "10-Step Process Toward Doing Your Job Successfully" checklist that is provided, demonstrate that you have completed each checklist item by placing an "X," check-mark, or other designation next to the completed item.

5. The completed *Job-Success Plan Workbook* and the "10-Step Process Toward Doing Your Job Successfully" checklist will be your job-success plan. Use this plan as a guide to ensure your job success.

6. Execute the plan that you have developed.

JOB-SUCCESS PLAN DEVELOPMENT
Write Your Answers in the Space Provided

STEP 1: DEFINE: WHAT IS YOUR JOB?
WHAT IS THE PURPOSE OF YOUR JOB?

Write your response in the box below

What are the stated job duties and responsibilities of your job? (You can find this information in your job description and from other sources). Do these match with your capabilities? If "no," there is a gap. Circle the gaps.

Job Duties	Is There a Match [Yes / No]	Job Responsibilities	Is There a Match [Yes / No]

Based on feedback and input from your manager, successful peers, and job predecessors, what are five key requirements for being successful in your job? If you don't feel you can complete these requirements and answer "no," there is a gap. Circle the gaps.

Job-Success Requirements	Can I Do This? [Yes / No]

STEP 2: PERFORM A GAP ANALYSIS

List all the gaps that you have identified (circled) above, and identify what is needed to close the gap(s). You must identify how you will close every gap.

Gaps	Needed to Close the Gap

GAP-CLOSING LEARNING, DEVELOPMENT, AND SUPPORT PLAN

Based on the things that you have identified as "needed to close the gap" in the table above, work with your manager to develop your actionable learning, development, and support plan to close the identified gaps.

Gaps	Type of Need	Needed to Close the Gap
	☐ Learning ☐ Development ☐ Support ☐ Other	
	☐ Learning ☐ Development ☐ Support ☐ Other	
	☐ Learning ☐ Development ☐ Support ☐ Other	
	☐ Learning ☐ Development ☐ Support ☐ Other	
	☐ Learning ☐ Development ☐ Support ☐ Other	
	☐ Learning ☐ Development ☐ Support ☐ Other	

STEP 3: ENSURE THAT YOUR OBJECTIVES ARE S.M.A.R.T.

Document each of your key job-related work objectives that are listed in your performance plan. If they are not S.M.A.R.T., then re-articulate them with the help and approval of your manager.

Though I recommend it, you do not need to include your behavioral or other subjective performance measures. However, it is a good idea to consider rearticulating those, too, in as S.M.A.R.T. a manner as possible.

Originally-Worded Objective	Rearticulated S.M.A.R.T. Objectives

STEP 4: DOCUMENT YOUR RE-ARTICULATED OBJECTIVES AND MAKE THEM VISIBLE

Document the rearticulated objectives from the table above and put them somewhere you can see them each day. For example, make them your computer screen-saver or print them out and put them on your desk, etc.

Where will you place them to ensure daily visibility?	

STEP 5: DEVELOP A PLAN FOR HOW YOU WILL ACHIEVE A "MAKE"

Because there may be multiple tasks required to complete an initiative or project, I recommend that you track the activities, tasks, and necessary to-dos to complete the initiatives/projects in an electronic source. It is also best practice to reproduce this "make" plan using an electronic tool, like a spreadsheet or document program, so that you can add additional initiatives/projects, and activities and tasks, as needed.

DEVELOPING YOUR "MAKE" PLAN

1. Ensure that "if-then" (cause-and-effect) logic is applied

When completing your plan and identifying tasks, ask the following two cause-and-effect questions: (1) if I successfully complete each of these tasks (cause), will it result in or contribute to the completion of the associated initiative (effect)? And (2) if I complete all the initiatives, will this result in the achievement of the associated objective?

If the answer to either question is "no," then you should define different sets of initiatives and tasks until the answer to both questions is "yes."

2. Complete the table (plan) below

(Recreate or make copies for additional table entries as needed)

Work Objectives	Initiatives and CSFs	Activities and Tasks**
Measurable determinants of your job success	The initiatives or projects or critical success factors that achieve the objective	The activities or tasks that must be completed to complete the Initiative
Objective #1	Initiative #Objective 1- Initiative 1	Task 1: Task 2: Task 3:
	Initiative # O1-2	Task 1: Task 2: Task 3:
Objective #2	Initiative #O2-1	Task 1: Task 2: Task 3:
	Initiative # O2-2	Task 1: Task 2: Task 3:

Objective #3	Initiative # O3-1	Task 1:
		Task 2:
		Task 3:
	Initiative # O3-2	Task 1:
		Task 2:
		Task 3:
Objective #4	Initiative # O4-1	Task 1:
		Task 2:
		Task 3:
	Initiative # O4-2	Task 1:
		Task 2:
		Task 3:
Objective #5	Initiative # O5-1	Task 1:
		Task 2:
		Task 3:
	Initiative # O5-2	Task 1:
		Task 2:
		Task 3:

** Each activity, task, or to-do should read specifically as an activity that must be performed. This should also include the anticipated completion date for the task.

3. Identify resources needed

For each initiative, determine the resources you will need to complete the initiative, project, or Critical Success Factors that you have defined.

Initiative	Resources Needed for Each Initiative
#	• •
#	• •
#	• •
#	• •
#	• •
#	• •
#	• •
#	• •
#	• •

STEP 6: PRIORITIZE YOUR WORK

Document your identified action items, tasks, and to-dos, and for each one, ask: "If I compete this task, will it get me a step closer to completing an initiative/project/critical success factor, or help me achieve an objective?" If the answer is "no," then the task is likely not a priority, and you should determine if it is worth the time and effort to complete it.

You can also ask: "What are the consequences if I do not complete this task?" If there are consequences for not completing the task, then the task may be considered important. Once you have identified important and/or priority tasks, add them to your calendar to ensure with a greater likelihood that they will get done.

Task	Important or Priority? [Yes / No]	Rank the "Yes" Tasks in Order of Importance

As required, use an electronic tool, such as a spreadsheet, document, or task list, so that you can add tasks to the list.

STEP 8: CONSTANTLY WORK TO IMPROVE YOUR SKILLS AND ABILITY

[Note: STEP 7 requires no documentation]

Repeat STEP 2 (using the same worksheets) and develop a market-skill gap

STEP 10: REWARD YOURSELF!

[Note: STEP 9 requires no documentation]

Create a list of rewards or things that bring you pleasure

Reward Options

JOB-SUCCESS PLAN CHECKLIST

10 STEPS TO DOING YOUR JOB SUCCESSFULLY	Complete?
STEP 1: UNDERSTAND WHAT YOUR JOB REALLY IS	
• Understand the true purpose of your job	
• Complete this sentence: If I do my job successfully, the value that I will provide to this organization is _____	
• Map your skills and experience against the job responsibilities to identify gaps	
• Understand whether or not you would be successful in the job if you **only** executed (successfully) the stated job requirements	
• Speak with your job's predecessors who have successfully performed the job, and learn	
STEP 2: UNDERTAKE AN HONEST INVENTORY OF YOUR CURRENT STATE AND PERFORM A GAP ANALYSIS	
• Perform a gap analysis	
• Document a comprehensive list of the job duties and responsibilities you are charged with performing this year	
• Take an honest inventory of your talent, ability, and skill	
• Identify and document the gaps that exist between the job duties and your capability to perform them	
• Determine what is needed for you to close the TAS-gaps and successfully perform the duties	
• Document what is needed and, working with your manager, develop an actionable learning and development plan	

STEP 3: ENSURE THAT THE OBJECTIVES YOU ARE CHARGED WITH ACHIEVING TO HAVE A SUCCESSFUL YEAR ARE S.M.A.R.T.	
• Do not sign off on or approve a performance plan if the work objectives that you are charged with achieving are not S.M.A.R.T.	
• For each objective, ask three questions: (1) "How much and by when," to help quantify them and define the time parameter; (2) "Is every parameter clearly defined and specific?" If not, clarify and make them specific; and (3) "Is the objective S.M.A.R.T.?"	
• Identify the important, priority activities on which you should spend your time	
STEP 4: DOCUMENT YOUR GOALS AND OBJECTIVES AND MAKE THEM VISIBLE; REVIEW THEM DAILY	
• Ensure that your goals are clearly articulated and your objectives are clearly defined and S.M.A.R.T.;	
• Document your goals/objectives so that they can be stored and retrieved	
• Place a copy of the goals/objectives in a place that you can look at them once a day	
• Use your goals and objectives to qualify your daily list of activities, tasks, and the to-dos and determine which are important; set priorities	
STEP 5: DEVELOP A PLAN FOR HOW YOU WILL ACHIEVE A "MAKE"	
• Develop a plan to "show a make"	
• Use the *Job-Success Plan Workbook* to create your plan	
• Identify Critical Success Factors / Initiatives	
• Apply "If-Then" logic (Cause-and-Effect)	
• Adjust the plan as needed	

STEP 6: WORK PRODUCTIVELY	
• Prioritize activities, tasks, and the to-dos by qualifying them	
• Reduce "busy work" and eliminate "brownie work"	
• Decrease productivity detractors	
STEP 7: BE DILIGENT	
• Listen intently and follow instructions	
• Hold yourself responsible for performing your job; don't place blame	
• Plan jointly with your co-workers	
STEP 8: CONSTANTLY WORK TO IMPROVE YOUR SKILLS AND ABILITY	
• Take responsibility for improving your job-skill, development, and growth	
• Create a job- and market-skill map	
• Work with your manager, Learning and Development team, mentors, and other successful workers	
• Establish periodic development and growth check-ins with your manager	
• Read	
STEP 9: SET UP RECURRING MEETINGS WITH YOUR MANAGER	
• Institute a regularly scheduled meeting or phone call between you and your boss	
• Capture potential topics daily to be discussed during your recurring meeting or call	

STEP 10: REWARD YOURSELF!	
• Reward yourself for completing important activities, tasks, to-dos, initiatives, projects, and CSFs; for achieving important milestones, goals, and objectives	
• Create a list of rewards or things that bring you pleasure	

INDEX

www.ingramcontent.com/pod-product-compliance
Lightning Source LLC
Chambersburg PA
CBHW031401180326
41458CB00043B/6562/J